HER LIFE & TIMES

and the New Theater of Fashion
by

BillyBoy*

with
dolls, documents & designs
from the
BILLYBOY* Collection

Crown Trade Paperbacks
New York

Grateful acknowledgment is given to the following people or groups for use of their material:

J. P. MASCLET: Pages 1 (top left), 6 (center and bottom), 7, 14, 24 (bottom left), 25 (bottom left), 27, 31, 32 (left and bottom right), 33, 34, 35, 36, 40 (right), 41, 43, 49 (bottom left), 50, 52, 54, 55 (top), 58 (top), 59 (top right), 60, 63 (bottom), 66 (top), 67, 68, 69, 70 (top right and bottom), 71 (top left, top right, and bottom left), 75 (bottom), 76, 79 (left), 80 (left), 82, 96, 88 (top right and bottom), 89, 91, 92, 93, 94 (top), 97 (bottom), 101, 104, 106, 107, 109 (right), 111, 112 (right), 114, 130, 138, 139, 140, 141, 142, 143, 144, 147 (right), 149 (top left, top right, and bottom left), 150, 151, 152, 153, 155 (top right), 156 (left and center), 157 (center), 158 (bottom), 160 (top left, top right, and bottom), 161, 162 (row 1 left, row 2, row 3, row 4), 163 (row 1 left, row 2, row 3 right), 164 (center, bottom), 165, 169 (left), 171 (bottom), 180 (left), 181 (bottom), 190 (left); VINCENT KNAPP: Pages 1 (bottom right), 6 (top), 8, 17, 19 (top), 20 (left), 21 (right), 23 (bottom), 26, 28, 30, 32 (top), 38, 47, 49 (top left), 53, 59 (bottom left), 65, 66 (bottom), 70 (top left), 71 (bottom right), 74, 79 (right), 80 (right), 81, 88 (top left), 102, 103, 108 (left), 109 (left), 118, 146, 149 (bottom right), 154, 155 (top left, bottom right, and bottom left), 156 (right), 157 (left and right), 159, 160 (center), 162 (top right), 163 (row 1 center and right, row 3 left and center, row 4), 164 (top), 166, 167, 168, 169 (right), 170, 171, (top), 172, 174, 175, 178, 179, 180 (top right and bottom right), 181 (top right), 182, 183, 184, 185, 186, 187, 188, 189, 190 (right), 191; MATTEL: Pages 11 (bottom left), 16 (bottom), 18, 25 (top left), 26, 27, 40 (bottom left), 44, 45 (bottom right), 48, 51 (top right), 55 (bottom), 56, 57, 61, 63 (top), 64, 75 (top), 78 (bottom), 83, 84, 85, 87, 95, 100, 113 (bottom), 115, 116, 119, 120, 121, 124 (top left and bottom left), 131, 137; BRITISH MATTEL: Page 123 (right); MICHAEL VON AULOCK: Page 11 (top left); MARK LYON: Pages 137, 158 (top), 173, 177, 181 (top left); MABA: Pages 124 (top right, bottom right), 125; ANDY WARHOL: Page 8; SAKS FIFTH AVENUE: Page 11 (right); HENRY CLARKE: Pages 16 (top), 25 (right); RENÉ GRUAU: Pages 23 (top), 130; THE BALENCIAGA CATALOGUE: Page 24 (top left); BRITISH VOGUE: Page 24 (bottom right); THE HOUSE OF DIOR: Page 24 (top right); DELL COMICS: Pages 42, 46, 72, 73; CLYDE SMITH: Page 51 (bottom); THE HAMLYN PUBLISHING GROUP: Page 59 (photograph of Marilyn Monroe from Marilyn Monroe by Janice Anderson © 1983 The Hamlyn Publishing Group); T. V. GUIDE: Page 97 (top); WARNER BROS. INC.: Page 108 (photograph of Robert Redford from Stars! by Daphne Davis © 1972 Warner Bros. Inc.); STEVE SCHAPIRO/ TRANSWORLD FEATURE SYNDICATE: Page 108 (photograph of Warren Beatty from Stars! by Daphne Davis © Steve Schapiro/ Transworld Feature Syndicate); WESTERN PUBLISHING: Pages 110, 113 (top); MEL ODOM: Page 127; STEPHEN SPROUSE: Page 129 ("Barbie Bomb" © 1986 by Stephen Sprouse); PATRICK SARFATI: Page 129 (photograph of Ken from Illusions © 1986 by Patrick Sarfati); FRENCH VOGUE: Page 134 (photograph of BillyBoy*'s Barbie by Serge Rivier © French Vogue); THE MAISON YVES SAINT LAURENT: Page 138 (photograph of Yves Saint Laurent by Guidotti); FRÉDÉRIC CASTET: Page 147 (sketch of Dior fur coat © 1985 Frédéric Castet); CHRISTIAN DIOR PARFUMS: Page 148 ("Jules" drawing); HERMÉS: Page 151 (sketch of Barbie in suit); ELLE MAGAZINE: Page 153 (photograph of Bettina by Chevalier); PETER SHIRE: Page 176 (Memphis watercolor of Barbie's house © 1985 Peter Shire); GEORGE SOWDEN: Page 176 (drawing of car © 1985 George Sowden); WERNER: Page 176 (drawing of Barbie © 1985 Werner); KEITH HARING: Page 187 ("Glowing Baby" design on Barbie's T-shirt © 1986 Keith Haring).

Copyright © 1987 by BillyBoy*
All photographs by Jean-Pierre Masclet, Vincent Knapp, Michael von Aulock, and Mark Lyon copyright © 1985 by BillyBoy*
Photographs on pages 137, 158 (top), 173, 177, and 181 (top left) © 1987 Mark Lyon
The New Theater of Fashion copyright © 1986 by BillyBoy*

Published by Crown Publishers, Inc., 201 East 50th Street, New York, New York 10022. Member of the Crown Publishing Group.

A detailed list of acknowledgments is located on page 192.

Crown Trade Paperbacks and colophon are trademarks of Crown Publishers, Inc.
The BillyBoy* logo is a registered trademark of BillyBoy*
BARBIE and related character trademarks are owned by and used under license from Mattel, Inc. © Mattel, Inc. 1987, 1992.

Manufactured in Hong Kong

Library of Congress Cataloging-in-Publication Data

Boy, Billy*.
    Barbie: Her story and the New Theater of Fashion.

    1. Barbie dolls—United States—History.   2. Fashions—United States—History.   3. Costume design—United States—History.   I. Title.
TS2301.T7B66   1987   688.7′221   86-24334

ISBN 0-517-59063-8

10 9 8 7 6 5 4 3 2 1

First Paperback Edition

Book Design by George Corsillo

Barbie™

Barbie ™

C O N T E N T S

OF FASHION — A Couturier's Scrapbook

rowing up with Wilma Flintstone and Betty Rubble, Lucy, Patty Duke, and a myriad of other pop heroines, I knew that when Barbie entered my life it was going to be a *long* relationship! She was the perfect one. The goddess long awaited. The endless search was over. My interest in fashion and sociology undoubtedly stems from this early encounter. It has evolved into a daily activity that is both professional and personal; my vocation of collecting my beloved Barbie and my work in American and European *haute couture* complement each other. This collection brings fascinating ideas, interesting personal stories, and great liberation to my imagination. It also brings me great pleasure, as Barbie particularly shows me how beautiful life really can be . . . how much good humor abounds! She symbolically removes all cynicism and inspires achievement in all aspects of life. She is also the best barometer of the last twenty-eight years of trends in current taste. For a fashion historian, Barbie tells the tale of everything from Fath-style sheath dresses and Balenciaga-inspired *tailleurs* to Biba mod minis and YSL type maxi-coats.

Bettina, the legendary and extremely groovy French fashion model, whom I am proud to have the honor of calling my best friend, was the archetypal fashion mannequin, and, not surprisingly, she and Barbie had a lot in common during Barbie's early years. Bettina was also the inspiration for the Barbie "Nouveau Théâtre de la Mode," which I designed for the first Barbie Retrospective in Paris in 1985.

By April 1986, the world was becoming delirious with "Barbiemania." Lengthy articles on our dazzling heroine appeared in newspapers and magazines in Japan, Australia, all of Europe (even Poland), and the United States. The United States saw feature articles in *Women's Wear Daily, New York* magazine, the *Chicago Tribune*, the *Washington Herald*, the *New York Times*, the *Los Angeles Times*, and many other journals. Even local papers from Chattanooga, Tennessee, to Anchorage, Alaska, wrote about Barbie. She was covered by every major television network in the world. People took her to their hearts, recalling the innocent doll they had grown up with. Some who might not have had a Barbie doll were charmed by her story. Children were overwhelmed, and their delight was contagious. It has been amusing to see children react to hundreds of Barbies together in a sort of "class reunion." Children have the remarkable capacity of seeing things clearly. Their open, uncensored reactions are invigorating.

It has now become fashionable to emulate Barbie. A Saks Fifth Avenue advertisement that stunningly resembles the Barbie doll I styled illustrates this well. Mannequins in Bloomingdale's windows wearing Vivienne Westwood's little-girlish fashions are six-foot-tall copies of the 1960 Ponytail Barbie, complete with molded "springolator" open-toed pumps.

The "Barbie on Tour" extravaganza in the United States continued my interest in Barbie. The Barbie Retrospective and New Theater of Fashion opened in the United States on February 10, 1986, at the Passenger Terminal at Pier 92 in New York City. UPI reported that Mattel, Inc., spent $1.5 million to create a multimedia experience for the collection and to unveil the "Imagi-nation Stations," a series of life-size Barbie environments that represented the current collection of Barbie theme dolls. The entertainment included two-story-high Barbie cutouts, smoke machines, a breakaway wall of TV monitors, holograms of Martians, an animated video of Barbie and the Rockers debuting "Born with a Mike in my Hand," and six models dressed as Barbie, including one that glowed in the dark.

It was a truly star-studded event and included androgynous punk designers from Manhattan's underground, toy distributors, and world-famous artists. Andy Warhol unveiled his Barbie masterpiece. Dolph Lundgren of *Rocky IV* fame and designers Emilio Pucci, Fernando Sanchez, Arnold Scaasi, Akira, Maripol, Patrick Kelly, Kenneth J. Lane, Christophe de Menil, Geoffrey Beene, and Jean-Charles Castelbajac all attended. Mel Odom, Calvin Churchman, and Brian Scott Carr showed up after having spent forty-eight hours setting up the exhibition.

There were young women dressed as Barbie in her "Solo in the Spotlight" outfit, as well as in her generic look. Mary Trasko, the journalist, wore a teased hairdo of mammoth proportions and was reported to have looked like "a freaked-out fashion queen." Trasko's friend, Steve Johanknecht, wore a "Golden Dream" Barbie around his neck as a pendant, as did a few other guests.

Barbie's illustrator, Clyde Smith, and his wife attended, as well as many well-known models including the beautiful Beverly Johnson. Paige Powell and Pat Hackett snapped a billion pictures. My main gal Friday, Jane X, and my assistants ran around madly greeting guests. The dazzling Bettina graciously met old and new friends from the fashion industry, while many of her photos graced the show. The more than thirteen hundred guests kept the party hopping until after 3:00 A.M.

It is by sheer luck and magic that I have the good fortune to have talented friends filled with imagination and exuberance. The dolls dressed by couturiers and artists amaze me in every respect. They are veritable masterpieces, delicate and captivating.

It is with great joy that, with the generous support of Mattel, Barbie's "parents," I have had the opportunity to show my collection to the world. Now, with this book, my greatest hope is that many more people will come to know and love Barbie. I hope readers enjoy it as much as I have enjoyed bringing it to them.

BILLYBOY* ™

A Saks Fifth Avenue advertisement features a model dressed strikingly like the Barbie I styled for the Paris show. The caption pays tribute to Coco, Jackie, and Barbie. Are surnames really necessary?

The French Barbie I styled for the New Theater of Fashion in 1985.

Sonia Rykiel and me at the opening of the New Theater of Fashion, Paris, 1985.

J'aime Coco, Jackie, and Barbie. My fluted crystal runneth over with Don Perignon in celebration of Tous Les Calecons' nouvelle couture. The wool jacket, $86, and skirt, $46. Cotton turtleneck, $34.

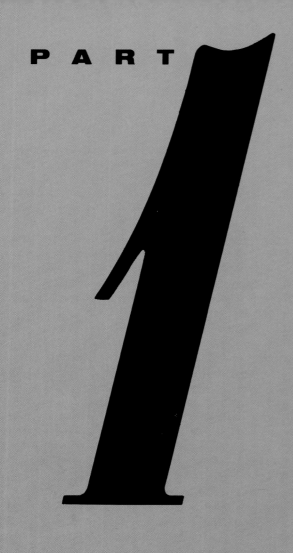

PART

1

Barbie™

HER LIFE & TIMES

Barbie, circa 1960,
wearing
"Commuter Set."

By 1950, Paris had not only begun to revive its war-ravaged self, but had magnificently reestablished its *haute couture* focus. Its new ruling stars were Dior and Fath. Other glittering members of the fashion constellation were Piguet, Dessès, Castillo, Cardin, Givenchy, Balmain, and Heim. Masters like Balenciaga and Schiaparelli were designing landmark innovations that would set the tone for the next decade. Chanel was to return soon to create her own revolution for the second time. Yves

The fabulous model Bettina as she looked in the 1950s. Her gown bears a startling resemblance to "Solo in the Spotlight."

The cover of the original Barbie catalogue. Note Barbie's flirtatious sidelong glance.

Saint Laurent would soon become artistic director at Dior, and he would create a sensation and a new emphasis on youth. Paris was the center again, and all roads led to her. It was into this rich environment that the world's first high-fashion doll made her debut.

Bettina, the startling Jacques Fath discovery, was the model all women hoped to resemble, if only just a little. She had short bobbed hair, arched and styled eyebrows, fire-engine-red lips, plus youth and a remarkably graceful, nonchalant set of gestures and expressions. In America, which still looked to France to tell it what to wear, young women took note of Bettina, an omnipresent force of fashion.

In the 1950s many aspects of culture were changing, and the education of children reflected these changes. It makes sense that a doll would be created that could capture completely and ideally the changes in aesthetics, fashion, and social values, as well as broader political and cultural trends. By 1959 that doll (the word stems from the Greek *eidolon*, "idol") had been created, and her name was Barbie.

Like Bettina, Barbie was a fashion model, young and pert. Actually, she was a "teenage fashion model." According to Bevis Hillier, in his recent book, *The Style of the Century 1900–1980*, the term *teenage* has a less than innocent connotation:

The very word "teenager" came to have a naughty glamour, like "flapper" in the twenties. It occurred in the hit song "Why must I be a teenager in love?" (pronounced "lerv" by American singers). Between 1956 and 1961, no fewer than eight movies had titles beginning with this word: Teenage Rebel *(1956),* Teenage Wolfpack *(1956),* Teenage Bad Girl *(1957),* Teenage Caveman *(1958),* Teenage Monster *(also titled* Meteor Monster*) (1959),* Teenagers from Outer Space *(1959),* Teenage Zombies *(1960),* and Teenage Millionaire *(1961). . . .*

Hillier does not point out, however, that in America there was a constant attempt to show young people as good role models. Commercials, television sitcoms, and movies showed the positive side of American youth. Singers and celebrities such as Frankie Avalon, Annette Funicello, Ricky Nelson, Paul Peterson of the *Donna Reed Show*, and the Everly Brothers and Connie Francis all showed the bright side of teen life.

Nineteen fifty-nine was the year that youth really began to make its mark on culture. The evidence was everywhere: Little Miss America contests, *Teenbeat* magazine, "Parfum à Go-Go" by Hattie Carnegie, and, of course, "Pepsi, for those who think young." *Teenage* would have a new meaning, and Barbie was a leading representative of its positive new definition.

On the cover of the little fashion booklet that accompanied this doll, her profile and side-glanc-

"Solo in the Spot-light," a dra-matic black glitter-gown accented with a rose, came with long black gloves, a pink scarf, a beaded necklace, and a microphone—perfect accoutrements for a glamorous torch singer. Almost all of Barbie's early ensembles were given whimsical appellations, reflecting the charming *haute couture* custom of naming outfits to evoke dreams.

ing eyes, set against a pink gouache background, suggested an air of remarkable sophistication. Her bright blond ponytail and saucy red lips suggested Americana and youth, while her discreet pearl earrings and choker insisted "Chanel." The painterly strokes of blue that indicated dress straps reminded one of the drawings of René Gruau. When one turned the page of this booklet, one entered a world of high fashion, culture, and fantasy that, with all the cynicism removed, made fashion a delightful experience for young people.

At the Toy Fair in New York in February 1959, Mattel introduced their new product with a great deal of enthusiasm. The Mattel catalogue exclaimed: "New for '59, the BARBIE doll: A shapely teenage Fashion Model! Retail price $3.00. . . ." The text went on prophetically to condense the entire projection of Barbie in later years: "An exciting all-new kind of doll (She's grown-up!) with fashion apparel authentic in every detail! This is Barbie—one of Mattel's proudest achievements for '59. Girls of all ages will thrill to the fascination of her miniature wardrobe of fine-fabric fashions: tiny zippers that really zip . . . coats with luxurious linings . . . jeweled earrings and necklaces . . . and every girl can be the star. There's never been a doll like Barbie. . . ."

Here's Barbie, 1959. The text for the early "Basic Barbie Doll Fashion Model Set" read: "Your Barbie Doll is made of sturdy flesh tone, vinyl plastic. Moveable arms, legs, and head make it easy to dress Barbie in her exciting fashion model's wardrobe. Barbie Doll, plus striped jersey swimsuit, sun glasses, pearl earrings, and shoes . . . and special pedestal to keep Barbie on her feet for all fashion shows. $3.00." Her box was illustrated with *haute couture*–style drawings. Her ensembles, such as "Roman Holiday Separates" and "Sweet Dreams" came with every accessory Barbie would ever need.

Barbie allowed a child to relate her child-size hopes and needs to the world of adults. She prepared a child for all the values that lay ahead without being too realistic and heavy-handed. By representing ideals of physique, social attitude, and aesthetics in design and fashion, Barbie allowed a child to learn at her own pace. Barbie's universe in 1959 was one that took only the graceful highlights of reality and made them a symbolic world full of fantasy.

Some believe that Barbie was fashioned after "Lilli," a German doll produced in the mid-1950s. Lilli was orginally conceived by the German cartoonist Reinhard Beuthien for the daily newspaper *Bild-Zeitung*, when they needed an emergency filler for the June 24, 1952 edition. The cartoon was originally meant to make a one-time appearance but the public adored Lilli. Beuthien's wife Erika gave him suggestions for Lilli's (or "his daughter," as he once referred to her) fashionable wardrobe. His credo was "I love to send up women but without portraying them as ugly or nasty—rather with warmth and humor." Lilli became very popular to the point of being honored in a Hamburg artist's club, *die insel*, by putting copies of the naïve darling on its walls. The cartoonist also created a second character almost identical to Lilli for the "Munchen Abendzeitung" newspaper called *Schwabinchen*. She had a different hairstyle than Lilli, but it was Lilli's success that brought about the idea of a three-dimensional doll version.

Although it took a number of proposals to meet the standards of Reinhard Beuthien, it was Max Weissbrodt, the creator of the fabulous Elastolin figures produced by O. & M. Hausser in Neustedt bei Coburg, who perfected her. A cooperation between Weissbrodt and the firm Griener and Hauser GmbH produced the heavy plastic doll. Under the management of Rolf Hauser, son-in-law of Mrs. E. Martha Maar, Lilli was put together and dressed by Drei-M-Puppenfabrik Maar KG in Monchsroden bei Coburg. It was Mrs. Maar who designed the entire Lilli packaging, an ovoid tube of clear plastic on a "Lilli" marked stand. She debuted on August 12, 1955 and was exported all over the world. She came with a miniature *Bild-Zeitung* newspaper, where the cartoon was available every Sunday in the real journal. Lilli was later manufactured in Hong Kong, and this version, sometimes called "Hong Kong Lilli" came in two versions, one Barbie-size, the other seven inches tall. Lilli's success however was short-lived and she was eventually sold to Mattel. Through the coordination of Jack Ryan, then Mattel executive, and Ruth and Elliot Handler, the remake of Lilli's image thus gave birth to Barbie. The "*Bild* Lilli" doll was a tall, slim, fashion model type of teenage girl. She had a lot in common with the newly popular movie star Brigitte Bardot, whose honest sexuality and startling frankness were hailed during

Barbie's presumed prototypes, the German *Bild* Lilli dolls: Hard, Harder, and Hardest.

The *Bild* Lilli doll was inspired by a popular cartoon from the German newspaper *Bild*.

Actress Brigitte Bardot (*above and right*) during her *yé-yé* years. Some people think Bardot was Barbie's human counterpart. Maybe.

The "*Bild* Lilli" doll (*left*) is thought to have been an inspiration for Barbie. In fact, some believe the original Barbie was made from Lilli's molds.

Here's Barbie, 1960. Casual, elegant, and absolutely fabulous!

the *yé-yé* years in France. Lilli and Bardot had blond ponytails and wore similar clothes. There may be a physical resemblance between Lilli, Bardot, and Barbie, but any further similarities are debatable.

Barbie, portrayed as a "teenage fashion model," had a wardrobe that, on the surface of the Barbie phenomenon, seemed to be the center of her lifestyle. Her clothes were based on the actual *haute couture* of the fashion leaders. The first twenty-one ensembles created for Barbie upon her launch, and nearly all in the years to follow, were designed at Mattel by the staff of Charlotte Johnson, later known as C.J., who would travel seasonally to Europe to watch the Paris collections. Dior, Fath, Heim, Balenciaga, Givenchy, Grès, Schiaparelli, Carven, Balmain, and Saint Laurent were all inspirations for the first few years of Barbie's extensive wardrobe. Her impeccably created garments had tiny buttons and zippers, and silk linings, which were coordinated with incredible accessories in high-fashion colors and sumptuous textiles.

Barbie's first set presented her dramatically. On an orange background of clouds, the pallid-skinned Basic Barbie, in her pinup-girl pose, waited to be dressed and placed in innumerable scenes. At that time, before the advent of women's liberation, little girls believed that they would grow up to be either mothers or high-fashion models, and they generally were not encouraged to aspire to much else. Barbie, as she evolved, changed with society and the roles little girls would emulate, but this Basic Barbie was the beginning of all that.

The first two outfits shown in the Basic Barbie booklet were undergarment sets, clothes that symbolize adulthood to most young girls. They allowed young women to anticipate the structured and difficult-to-wear undergarments of the era. In the late 1950s, the girdle was a necessary garment that supposedly encouraged good posture (as Barbie exemplified with her completely straight back). Girdles were also necessary attachments for hosiery. Panty hose, invented by Mary Quant, did not become fashionable until the sixties.

In the March 1959 issue of *Harper's Bazaar,* an all-important couture issue entitled "The Eyes On Paris and America," several pages devoted exclusively to undergarments claimed: "The new spring clothes rely increasingly on a lean, defined (as opposed to pinched) upper torso and waist. Nearly all of us will need a new kind of control to achieve this. . . . Some clothes may well exact special measures of corsetry." As one woman commented on the subject, "When you're a young girl, this is all new to you. Dressing your Barbie doll helped you to figure it out; all the private or embarrassing questions found simple and elegant answers at a pace suited to your curiosity."

Although the Barbie doll is accused of having an

In these Schiaparelli designs from 1959, we see more than a hint of Barbie in both the Schiaparelli fashions and the illustrator's interpretation.

abnormally proportioned body, this is not true at all. She has the ideal that Western culture has insisted upon since the 1920s: long legs, long arms, small waist, high round bosom, and long neck. Her first underwear sets, like her graceful body, simply reflected current standards of feminine beauty.

Barbie's breasts have been an almost absurd topic of discussion. "It was the TITS. After all, that's what being an adult meant, wasn't it? I loved Barbie's so much. Whenever I put another outfit on her it was just to see how they'd look in it," said Carol, a magazine editor, in an article in the *Village Voice* entitled "Boobs in Toyland." (It is also important to note that Barbie was originally billed as a "3-D fashion drawing" which accounts for her long stylized figure and *poetrine*.) Ruth Handler, Barbie's creator, claimed, ". . . Barbie was originally created to project every little girl's dream of the future," and, if only for 1959, that dream included this maturity of figure.

In the early 1950s, Balenciaga designed the fabulous red coat, illustrated above by the noted fashion artist Gruau. "Red Flair" (1962–1965) pays absolute homage to the Spanish designer, yet at the same time, "Red Flair" is also reminiscent of the Trapeze line Yves Saint Laurent designed for Dior during the same era.

Créée
pour
la
ligne
Dior
la gaine Christian Dior
GAINES ET CORGES

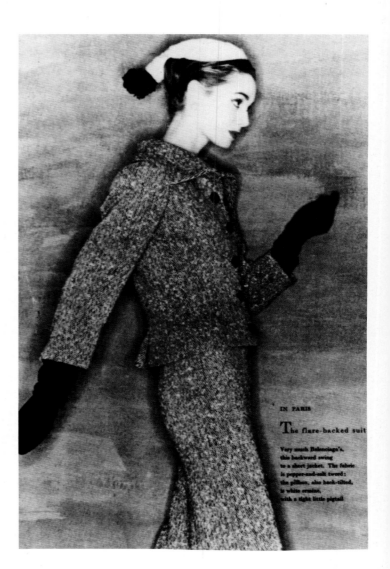

Balenciaga's flair-backed suit in "pepper-and-salt tweed" *(right)* un-doubtedly inspired "Career Girl" *(left)*, designed for Barbie in 1963. Balencia-ga's black suit with white ermine collar (1958), illustrated by Nino Caprioglio, also evokes a similar, though perhaps more formal, feeling.

BASIC BARBIE DOLL FASHION MODEL SET

Your Barbie doll is created of sturdy flesh-tone vinyl plastic. Moveable arms, legs and head make it easy to dress Barbie in her exciting fashion model's wardrobe. Barbie Doll, plus striped jersey swimsuit, sun glasses, pearl earrings and shoes...and special pedestal to keep Barbie on her feet for all Fashion Shows. $3.00

Notice the remark- able similarity be- tween the well-known French lingerie adver- tisements created for Dior by René Gruau *(opposite)* and the poses Barbie struck to model her early garments.

Christian Dior surely inspired "After Five" (1962–1964).

In a recent controversial court case, covered in a battery of articles, Barbie's breasts became a focal point. The doll was produced in court as evidence in defense of the "Shirtless Seven," who were prosecuted for baring their chests in public. Several women had pre-publicized an event in which they would remove their shirts and bras in protest to the inequity in the law relative to shirtless men as opposed to shirtless women. This issue, which one would have presumed was resolved in the seventies, reared its ugly head and the protesters were duly arrested for "public exposure." After a lot of legal gobbledegook, Barbie was used as a scapegoat by a clinical psychologist who claimed many women suffer mentally and physically while trying to achieve a Barbie-like figure. She was accused of being "gravity-defying" while the defense argued that the breast is not a sexual object and that the New York State ordinance violates women's rights to equality under the fourteenth amendment. Fortunately some reasonable and considerate commentators came forth. Women's rights leader Betty Friedan said "It is not very serious" and that it was a classic issue of second-stage feminism. Mrs. Handler, now sixty-nine years old, came even more to the point by saying, "In my opinion people make too much of breasts. They are just part of the body" and then vented her indignation against "nasty adult minds."

At the time of Barbie's debut, slumber parties were the rage for girls, and Barbie's sleep ensembles showed teenage spirit as well as a very high-fashion influence. Pierre Balmain was at this time producing "Jolie Madame" lingerie known throughout the world. Meanwhile, in America, the lingerie manufacturer Rogers exclaimed of its nylon lingerie set: "Every man wants his woman on a pedestal, Rogers places you there in miles of dreamy softness, counting pleat upon pleat to dreamland." Barbie's sleepwear had a touch of this fashion romance.

The next outfits in the Barbie booklet pertained to hygiene and homemaking, two subjects that were stressed in the education of teenagers, and became almost a cliché of late 1950s American households (your basic Donna Reed syndrome!). Owners saw Barbie readying herself for sleep, getting dressed, and grooming herself, all important for a sound and healthy body. By the presentation of these good standards, Barbie set the right example. Her attitude toward cleanliness made it seem like a pleasant and cheerful experience, something to look forward to. Homemaking, a bourgeois role traditionally handed down from mother to daughter, now also acquired new elegance and style. The pink dress that accompanied Barbie's "Barbie-Q" set reflected the current fashion tendency toward a small waist and huge full skirt, very much in the manner of Carven, Maggy Rouff, and the very youth-oriented Jacques Heim.

Barbie fashions reflected pure style, and were completely an American interpretation of French fashion. Paris designers were unknowingly influencing a whole generation of American Barbie doll owners through the very particular couturier details of Barbie's wardrobe. For example, all Barbie's ensembles had names, such as "Solo in the Spotlight," "Gay Parisienne," and "Roman Holiday Separates." This custom of giving outfits romantic names is one of the principal charms of French *haute couture*. Ensemble names were introduced in the mid-nineteenth century by Charles Frederick Worth and later by Doucet, and continued in the twentieth century by Paul Poiret. Naming garments was a way to evoke dreams that reflected tendencies of the epoch or whims of the designer. Mostly, they conjured up charming images that were pleasant to associate with the mood of the garment.

Barbie's lingerie combined high-fashion styling with pre-pubescent romance. Note the references to Parisian high fashion on the back of the box, then consider the amusingly naïve accoutrements.

"SWEET DREAMS"

(without doll) #973
Novelty tricot Baby
Doll gown and panties
trimmed with
embroidery and satin
bows. Hair bow to
match. Pastel
bedroom scuffs. Plus
Barbie's "Dear Diary"
book, her apple-a-day,
and alarm clock to
wake her in the morn!
Complete set, $1.25

#973

Diary

NIGHTY-NEGLIGEE SET

(without doll) #965
Luxurious full-length
tricot gown, Grecian
bodice with
embroidered flower.
Matching peignoir of
finely tucked tricot
with embroidered
pocket. Toy stuffed
dog for Barbie's bed.
The set. $3.00.

#965

Barbie's first "season" included outfits with titles that spanned morning to dazzling evening ensembles. "Midnight Blue" (1964), in silver and blue satin, created a typical Balenciaga silhouette. A sleeveless cape with a long train and fur collar covered a silver lamé bustier gown with a skirt of the same blue satin. The long gloves and silver lamé clutch were accessories Balenciaga often used. The pillbox hat made famous by Jacqueline Kennedy was also a genius creation of Balenciaga. "Reception Line" also included a pillbox, in baby blue taffeta. The text describing this outfit referred to Barbie's greeting royalty and "First Ladies."

"Gay Parisienne" (1959) interpreted Hubert de Givenchy's 1956 fashion thrill, the bubble dress, in polka-dotted silk taffeta. At about this time, Balenciaga, Cardin, Saint Laurent, Capucci, and Jacques Fath all created bubble dresses, each designer adding his particular styling. "Roman Holiday Separates" (1959) made its reference to the new trend of Italian *haute couture* that was just becoming familiar to the world press, aided in its popularity by the opinionated and daring Bettina Ballard of *Vogue* fame.

Barbie's early ensembles paid homage to the glories of French fashion. Outfits such as "Saturday Matinee" (1965) and "Gold 'N Glamour" (1965) showed the obvious influence of the House of Dior's designer Marc Bohan. Tailored suits displaying jackets with extended collars were typical of this designer's current style. The tweed interspersed with gold lamé was similar to what Abraham, BuCol, and Dormeuil were creating at the same time for use by the French *haute couture*.

The quality of the garments and their attention to detail are almost legendary, the most obvious details being the real silk or cotton full linings and hand-finished seams and hems. Buttons were sewn on by hand; hooks and eyes, zippers, and snaps were expertly set in. The pockets were real and well finished; the collars were lined the way real collars should be. Labels just like couturier labels were woven with the Barbie logo signature and were neatly sewn into Barbie's dresses. Ken's clothes had their labels sewn onto the sides of the jackets, where one finds them in finely tailored menswear. Skirts had a small skirt-hanger strap on each side. Minute pleating, fabric weaves, ribbon bows, buckles, and trims were important details. These early garments were produced by cottage industry in Japan. Because they had not been mass-produced, each group of pieces had a very couture finish.

The latest innovations in fabrics were also evident in Barbie's clothing. To create these first outfits, nylon tricot was employed, a light-textured synthetic frequently used during the mid-1950s. This fact was emphasized in the text of the Barbie catalogue, as nylon tulle, sheer nylon, and nylon net were used in many of her outfits.

Helanca, the company that created the stretchy jersey of the same name, was immortalized in Barbie's "Helanca Swimsuit" of 1962–1963. This company was among the first to create tights. Later, Mary Quant and Valentino would use this innovation creatively. Tights appeared in Barbie's world as early as 1961, then again in 1962 and 1963 in a stretch synthetic. Later, during the "Quant era," nearly every ensemble included tights in Lurex, a new metallic fabric, or wild psychedelic prints.

Barbie's accessories, jewels, and "Fashion Frosting" were the height of fashion, such as a pearl necklace to match a black sheath and white gloves, a pearly pendant for a bouncy chintz dance dress, a wraparound snake bracelet of pearls, and shimmering "à la Calder" charm bracelets for a "Resort Set." The Sew Free outfits of 1964 contained stunning bracelets of Veniniesque stones to become parure with necklaces of alternating crystal, ruby, and jet. There was also Kenneth J. Lane–inspired jewelry which came as pak items and licensed accessory kits.

The Cleinman and Sons of Rhode Island set, produced in 1962, is a very good example of Barbie's fabulous accessories. It came with little-girl-size copies of the Barbie-size jewels. The text on the box was exciting: "Thrill to your very own glamorous Barbie jewelry. These lovely 'look alike' sets for both you and Barbie are designed and made just like the very finest costume jewelry worn by the world's most beautiful and glamorous women. . . ." This text illustrates that during this epoch it was considered *de rigueur* to be well accessorized at all times.

Barbie even had nifty glitter-trimmed harlequin glasses and eyeglass case, a spiffy "B"-initialed compact, and a minuscule cotton hanky.

Barbie's shoes were also fashionable to an extreme. The famous Barbie open-toe pump is reminiscent of those worn by Hollywood starlets. Some shoes even had pompoms or glitter on them. The pointy-closed-toe high-heeled pump, which came in such colors as ecru, bone, aqua, lime, raspberry, and clear with glitter, was a tribute to its real Italian couture version of the 1960s. She even had gold-trimmed cork wedgies. Barbie's boots, which were in the style of Herbert Levine, David Evins, and Delman, later evolved into those made famous by Nancy Sinatra of "These boots are made for walking" fame. Barbie's footwear later took on a Mary Quant and Courrèges look in baby-pale acid tones of green, pink, and yellow.

Yet from the start, although Barbie was the height of fashion, she was always much more than that. Quickly she revealed a whole personality—and a host of emotions, professions, likes (and, rarely, dislikes), and hobbies. She became the personification of the all-around American girl.

Here's Barbie wearing a new hairstyle and a bellskirt evening dress, "Golden Evening," which came with a scintillating charm bracelet. It was in *Barbie's New York Summer* by Cynthia Lawrence (1962) that Barbie first cut her hair into a casual bubble-cut style. The Jacques Heim dress on the right is very similar to some of Barbie's bellskirt dresses. The Heim model also sports a bubble cut—everything just like Barbie—except for the cigarette.

VACA

For "Open Road," "Barbie takes the High Fashion road, with beige sweater, striped pants, and car coat fastened with real leather straw hat tied with scarf and has toggles and real toggles match. A map shows the way to fun." The set is extremely Bonnie Cashin and looks straight out of American *Vogue*, 1959. It also resembles clothes in *Elle* or *Marie Claire* from the same period, especially the hat, which has a decidedly Givenchy shape.

TION!

The impeccably tailored, cuffed blue jeans in "Picnic Set" were topstitched in the yellow thread typical of the late 1950s. There is something tomboyish about this outfit, right down to the fishing pole, but it also exudes a high-style, feminine line.

Daytime G

"Resort Set" (1959–1962) with middy jacket, striped shirt, and sharp white short-shorts could take Barbie from Côte d'Azur to Palm Beach.

The knitted outfits, such as "Sweater Girl" *(right)*, "Knitting Pretty," and "Square Neck Sweater," were perfectly scaled with meticulously ribbed cuffs and waists.

Early jewelry designed for Barbie *(opposite)* in the style of Gripoix and the best of Parisian "toc."

l'amour

"Winter Holiday" (1959) made reference to the new trend of "nouvelle vague" that was just becoming popular for teenagers.

"On the Avenue," *(above)* sometimes known as "Sunday Visit," recalled Balenciaga's short flyaway jacket. This outfit was made of wool Lurex weave in cream and gold. It combined a sheath, typical of Balenciaga, with a jacket semibelted in the front with gold kid. **A**nother early ensemble that glorified French fashion, "Evening Splendor" (1959; *right*), an exciting sheath and long coat of gold brocade, showed the obvious influence of the most famous Parisian couturiers.

Dazzling

Evening

"**E**nchanted
Evening" (1960–
1963) was one of the
first—and ultimately
one of the most re-
membered—evening
gowns designed for
Barbie and reflected
the classical elegance
of Dior. The touch of fur
evokes the glamour of
Marlene Dietrich and
Marilyn Monroe.

GENUINE
TEEN AGE FASHION MODEL™ *Barbie*®
BY MATTEL

Barbie® GENUINE
TEEN AGE FASHION MODEL™
BY MATTEL

"Plantation Belle" was a full organdy number with capeline hat, elaborate jeweled day bag, and pale pink pearl accessories.

Barbie's packaging reflected all the elegance of Parisian couture advertising.

Barbie's World

he early 1960s marked a high point for traditional family life. Television shows such as *Father Knows Best* with Robert Young and Jane Wyatt, showed the average American family in strong unity and emphasized the close relationship between all the members. After Barbie's high-fashion launch, the next years projected her vital relationships with family and friends.

Ken, created in 1961, was Barbie's boyfriend, introduced with the exquisite double entendre

"He's a doll," a typical American expression of the period indicating his attractiveness. Ken stood twelve inches tall. His physique was particularly noteworthy, as it was typical in Western culture of this period. Often accused of being skinny and too pale, Ken did not divulge any of the sexual secrets that the near-pubescent girl might care to discover. In fact, the first generation of Barbie owners boast of defeating Ken sexually, either with their Barbie dolls or with complicated fantasies. But basically Ken's image was a healthy blend of innocence, cleanliness, extroverted playfulness, and, most important, *boyish* masculinity, with a hint of shyness. He looked like Dwayne Hickman, the lovelorn Dobie Gillis from the TV show of the same name. Ken's blue eyes looked straight ahead, hinting at his directness, not only with Barbie, but with all teenage dreamers.

Ken now lent Barbie's world the possibility of romance, companionship, and even marriage, as the last page of the Barbie booklet showed the "Wedding Day Set," a lush "Balmain-esque" full gown in satin, lace, and tulle. The set even came with a blue garter for good luck. This detail was significant in that it reinforced the traditional American values portrayed in this early period of Barbie's evolution. One woman, in an article on Barbie, claimed, "I made Mom drive around in the station wagon to all the shopping centers to get the wedding dress—that was the best outfit, because it was the most expensive."

Ken's outfits were of high quality and excellent tailoring, like "Campus Corduroy" (1964; *right*) and "Dream Boat" (1962; *opposite*). In the early days, Ken's outfits leaned toward the conservative, "Ivy" image and came with appropriate accessories. The map in Ken's pocket actually came as part of another landmark outfit, "Rally Day" (1962), which also included tiny keys for a sports car.

The 1961 catalogue (*left*) first introduced Ken, referring to him as Barbie's "handsome steady."

The first television commercial for Ken, in the early months of 1961, was an absolutely charming ministory. It was filmed in black-and-white, set against a stylized ballroom in which the vague silhouettes of women in ball gowns evoked both 1890 and 1960. Barbie was in a draped pink satin gown, "Enchanted Evening," with a white fur stole. The ballroom music swelled. A sultry female narrator set the romantic scene: "It all started at the dance. . . ." Using animation, the Barbie doll turned her head and glanced back as the camera panned to the side to discover a hazy silhouette in the distance: Ken in a tuxedo. The music swelled. "She met Ken! . . . Somehow Barbie knew that she and Ken would be going together." The commercial went on to explain that Ken was Barbie's new boyfriend and that they had many coordinated outfits for beach, fraternity dances, after-school sodas, and all the other things young couples enjoyed in 1961. The commercial's last sequence urged the viewer to "get Barbie and Ken and see where the romance may lead. . . ." The camera, in a close-up, created a splendid wedding-day album portrait of the teenage couple in the "Wedding Day Set" and "Tuxedo."

It is interesting to note that even though Barbie and Ken, according to Mattel spokespeople, never were to have married, the text of the Barbie booklet for "Wedding Party" (1965) claimed that her trousseau was for "All the romance of a big formal wedding and a dream honeymoon" and that Ken was "the handsome groom." The couple was shown posing before what appears to be a Christian altar. "Barbie's Wedding Party" even came with a tiny gold wedding ring on a satin ring bearer's pillow.

Whether he was an escort or a spouse, Ken's outfits were of high quality and excellent tailoring, with the usual attention to detail. "Rally Day" even included tiny keys for Ken's sports car and a map of California with an arrow showing Mattel's home, Hawthorne.

The relationship between Barbie and Ken was accentuated by the merchandising techniques and accessories. At this time, *Barbie* magazine ran stories of this teenage couple, such as "Barbie's First Prom." The story started with Barbie disturbed at the idea of her cousin Lulu Belle Rawlins from New Orleans coming to town just as the prom was to take place. Barbie hadn't seen her cousin in four years. " 'But I am one of the Princesses of the Prom,' " Barbie told her mother, worried. " 'Maybe I'll be crowned Queen that night. I won't have a minute to see if Lulu's having a good time, and you know how shy she is!' " However, Lulu was no longer her old shy self, but a beautiful, elegant, well-dressed southern charmer. To Barbie's surprise, and slight jealousy, Ken and Lulu Belle hit it off. Then, on the night of the prom, "Both girls looked every inch a Princess. 'Boy, look at Lulu!' Ken grinned. 'She's going

"He's a Doll!"

"**B**arbie and Ken" comic book–like magazines published by Dell in the early 1960s included fantasies of the glamorous couple's social whirl, from school dance to European Grand Tour (unescorted?) to live stage appearance! They have always been the glamorous twosome!

to make a lot of us YANKEE boys join the Confederacy tonight, huh, Barbie?' " Ken's reaction only furthered Barbie's jealousy.

At the prom, Ken and Lulu disappeared, and Barbie's evening turned into a nightmare. Even when Barbie was crowned queen (an event that Mattel would commemorate in a board game), she was full of despair, anger, and embarrassment. Suddenly Ken, Lulu, and Lulu's mother appeared with a real golden filigree tiara to replace the paper crown Barbie had worn. (They had gone out to the car to get it, and been delayed because they took the wrong set of keys!) Barbie then realized a valuable lesson. " 'I always want to keep both of these crowns. I never want to forget tonight, and how I found out that I spent a whole jealous week only deserving this fake crown. But in one evening a friend helped me to have the right to wear the real one.' "

This story is typical of those created around Barbie, giving her a realistic suburban American personality. They divulged important details about Barbie's home life, which increased her personal dimension. Her last name, Roberts, and her mother's first name, Margaret, were details that made her seem more like a real (albeit stunningly gorgeous) person.

Also enhancing Barbie and Ken's relationship were the illustrations on the carrying cases. They were sophisticated and romantic, yet somehow naïve, as they depicted typical American teenage scenes geared to children's fantasies of what adult life was like. These renditions were exacting in their representation of current graphics trends on Madison Avenue and high-fashion illustration in Paris. They were obviously influenced by the leader, Gruau, and other famous illustrators of the time, such as Eric, Pierre Simone, P. Morgue, and even Vertés. The final effect, however, conjured up thoughts of suburban lawn parties and teenage drive-ins, and were dense in their depiction of the type of taste found in department store advertising on Long Island, in downtown Chicago, or in Los Angeles suburbs. The style of these illustrated cases was charged with glamor, nonetheless. "Solo in the Spotlight" (1960–1964) comes to mind.

Music plays an important role in the history of Barbie. Her ambiance—the ultimate teenage dream life—was so beautifully projected in much pop music that many popular music classics since 1959 evoke her. Barbie was born the same year Phil Spector created the "wall of sound." While Barbie made her first appearances on the *Mickey Mouse* show alongside the Mouseketeers, Phil Spector's first hit was aired on Dick Clark's *American Band Stand*. Carol Connors struck a rather Barbie-dollish attitude in her rendition of "To Know Him Is to Love Him," with the Teddy Bears as her backup.

In 1961, for the first time Barbie fans could hear

Barbie's voice singing about her new boyfriend: "I never bothered with romance, or gave any boy a second glance, and then, I met Ken. . . ." In a very Julie London (on key) style, Barbie sang about the different situations common to young romances. A song called "The Busy Buzz" concerned jealousy. A girl calls her boyfriend, finds the line busy, and fantasizes that he's talking to another girl. "Now when I get that busy buzz, I'm not jealous like I used to be, 'cause while I'm busy buzzin' you, I know you're busy buzzin' me!"

This record was an important shaper of Barbie's personality. The reassuring voice reinforced her image as a real teenager, a fantasy sister to her owner, even a projection of the child's desires and ideas of adult life. The voice helped the child understand social manners, also. The social games prevalent during the early sixties (such as coyness and aloofness in teen relationships, for example—should you kiss on a first date?) were evident in the lyrics of this record.

Is it necessary to portray these social qualities in a doll, one might ask. It is of course debatable whether Barbie's personality contributed to women's rights. For good or bad, Barbie's personality was based on qualities that were present in society. That is, Barbie's personality reflected larger cultural attitudes. She was characterized as an average personality, and the most innocent qualities of courtship during this period were built into her image. It is these traits in Barbie that certain people have unjustly termed "unliberated" and "antifeminist." Some even portray Barbie as a victim of a man-oriented society and a sex object. This is a gross exaggeration. Perhaps Barbie was sexy; and, of course, being a doll, she was an object! But she was never a sex object. Society *made* Barbie, literally and figuratively. She reflected women's roles, but these roles were about to change radically, in part due to innovations in birth control and the refinement of mass communications. Barbie's world, like ours, was destined to evolve.

The *Barbie Sings!* record cover.

the busy buzz

Notice how the lyrics to "My First Date" reflected every little girl's fantasy of a romantic teenage life.

The artwork that accompanied the lyrics to "The Busy Buzz" record. Incidentally, Barbie's first telephone came in the famous design by Henry Dreyfuss. Later she used, appropriately, the "Princess."

my first date

I have one special favorite dream
As most folks do.
I turn out the light,
And most ev'ry night...
My favorite dream comes true.

I dream of my very first date...
And I feel so light,
I could dance all night,
Never touching the floor.
I dream that I'm staying out late...
And the boys all sigh
As I'm dancing by
With the one I adore.
Then it's midnight,
And like poor Cinderella, my dream castles fall...
After midnight,
It's just me and my pillow rememb'ring it all.
Some day, if I only can wait –
I'll be there, really there,
Wide awake – on my very first date!

A record case bearing homage to our girl.

BARBIE'S

In an early story, little Patty tells her friends that she knows Barbie and Ken are married because she attended the wedding. (Note, too, that Patty's fantasy includes the possibility of romance for herself.)

Barbie and her rather dazed bridegroom.

Barbie

TEEN-AGE FASHION MODEL

MATTEL INTERNATIONAL

BARBIE "WEDDING DAY" SET
Magnificent formal wedding gown with train and flowing veil. Satin bodice; flowered-net skirt over petticoat. Tricot gloves, blue garter, bouquet and wedding shoes.
Stock #972 (without doll). Retail: $5.00
Std. Pack: ½ doz. Wt., 3 lbs.

A NEW KIND OF DOLL FROM REAL LIFE...BY MATTEL!

"Barbie's 'Wedding Day' Set" featured in 1959 (*above*), and the later "Barbie's Wedding Party" (*opposite*) and "Wedding Party" doll case of 1965, suggested that Ken and Barbie were actually married.

Ken in a very elegant top hat and tails from 1965.

"I made Mom drive around in the station wagon to all the shopping centers to get the wedding dress— that was the best outfit, because it was the most expensive."

BARBIE-Q OUTFIT

(without doll) #962
Cotton sunback dress
with Chef hat and apron.
Barbecue cooking
utensils and potholder.
Summer shoes. The
set, $2.00.

962

Contains everything you need to make your own Barbie Costume

3 EASY STEPS!

1. APPLY MATTEL SEW-FREE STRIPS™
2. CUT OUT
3. PRESS TOGETHER WITH YOUR FINGERTIPS!

A WHOLE NEW WORLD OF FASHION WITHOUT SEWING A STITCH!

MATTEL, INC. TOYMAKERS®

"Sew-Free Fashion Fun" kit. Barbie looks not unlike Patsy Cline.

Barbie was always proficient at ultra-feminine homemaking arts—perfect skills for the perfect "wife." Her Barbie-Q outfit was a "cotton sunback dress with Chef hat and apron. Barbecue cooking utensils and potholder" provided Barbie with everything she needed to carry her homemaking out of doors.

Clyde Smith was one of the original illustrators for early books about Barbie, such as *Barbie's Fashion Success*, *Barbie's Hawaiian Holiday*, and *Barbie Solves a Mystery*. The cover of *Barbie's Easy Cookbook (right)* illustrates vividly Smith's youthful and lively style.

51

Midge wearing "Friday Night Date," a dress she borrowed from her pal Barbie, which apparently she wore on Saturday night.

MIDGE

arbie was having great success, with perhaps the only drawback being the tremendous sexuality portrayed through her high-fashion image (high fashion being a sophisticated aspect of sexual attractiveness). In 1963, Barbie's image was softened by the introduction of her best friend, Midge. Midge was exactly the same size as Barbie but less glamorous, and certainly less intimidating. Midge had a wider face, freckles, green eyes, and a flip hairdo. She represented the girl next door. If little girls found it difficult to relate to Barbie, they could certainly relate to Midge. Now Barbie owners could create more play situations. Midge was somehow more innocent and girlish than Barbie. She gave a dimension of friendliness to Barbie's personality and reduced the idea that Barbie was unapproachable.

The first Midge commercial introduced not only Midge, but also Barbie's dream house. The doorbell rings and "Surprise! It's Midge," smartly dressed in "Red Flair" (1962–1965). A ministory explains that Midge is Barbie's best friend; they go everywhere together, and "Midge is thrilled with Barbie's new career as a teenage model. . . ." She loves to try on all the high-fashion gowns that Barbie models because, the commercial insists, they are "exactly the same size." We even learn that Midge's last name is Hadley, through the Random House "Barbie" series of teenage novels.

There is only one discrepancy about Midge that is apparent in the May–June 1962 issue of *Barbie* magazine. In a cartoon called "Barbie, Teenage Fashion Model," Barbie, Ginnie (probably not the well-known doll by Vogue), and Midge go shopping:

Midge: *I wish I had your figure, Barbie. I'm just too short and round to look good in clothes.*

Ginnie: *Don't complain, what if you were a beanpole, like me?*

Barbie: *Oh, no one has a perfect figure. What you really have to do is learn some fashion tricks. Let's go to the store and I'll show you.*

(at the store)

Barbie: *Midge, you want to look taller and slimmer. Why don't you try a dress like Ginnie's, all up and down stripes!* (to Ginnie) *You need to make people look across, not up and down! A skirt and blouse in different colors and a wide belt in a third color takes away that height—and you look rounder, too!*

Midge to Ginnie: *Why, you look so different!*

Ginnie to Midge: *You do too!*

Barbie: *Oh! dear, the store's about to close, and I haven't bought a thing for myself.*

(later)

Mrs. Roberts: *Why, Barbie, weren't you going to get a new dress for your date tonight?*

Barbie: (laughing) *Mother, sometimes I think I know too much for my own good.*

A fabulous rare Midge without freckles (circa 1963; *right*) and an equally rare Midge *(below)* bearing a rather toothy grin.

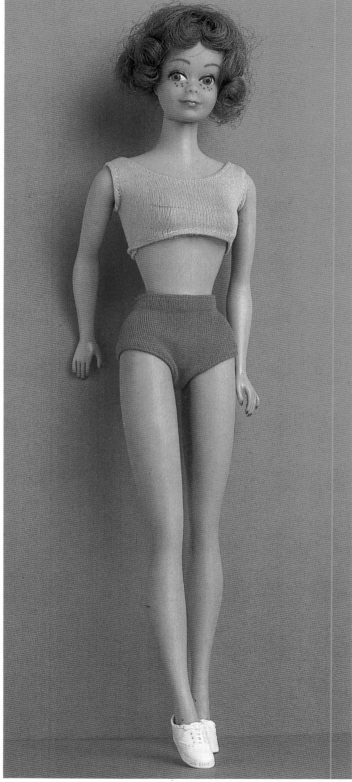

SKIPPER

Skipper, Barbie's little sister, arrived in 1964. Here she is wearing "Dress Coat" (1964), an outfit any girl whose Mom shopped at Best & Company will recognize—right down to the patent leather Mary Jane shoes.

This story is puzzling if we remember that Midge is supposed to be the same size as Barbie. Perhaps she was so impressed with Barbie's advice that she actually grew taller and lost weight in those few short months before her official launch as Barbie's best friend. Or perhaps Barbie's fashion advice worked so well that Midge created the illusion of being Barbie's size.

Midge became a great equalizer and confidante, not only for Barbie and the imaginary play situations, but also for doll owners. Cleverly, Mattel created the dolls in many hair colors, enabling parents or children to choose hair colors corresponding to those of friends and family. The possibility of creating associations between actual family situations and a child's Barbie family creatively reinforced the idea of family unity. Which brings us to Skipper, Barbie's little sister, introduced in 1964.

Skipper was nine and one-quarter inches tall and had a completely sexless body, which would later be used for her male companion, Ricky. She wore long, straight waist-length hair and the then-popular brass hair band with bangs. If the expression "cute as a button" ever applied, it was to Skipper. This doll proposed new play situations stemming from her elementary-school activities. Essentially, she offered a young girl's imagination the idea of growing up. She was closer in age to the child than was Barbie, and she represented the possibility of growing up to be as lovely as Barbie. Children related well to this idea. As one Skipper owner explained, "Barbie was distant; she had a boyfriend, she had a car, and, of course, those mysterious breasts. But Skipper was a friend, and I adored her long hair." One of the first commercials for Skipper, in 1965, explains that "She's just like you"—she likes ice cream, roller skating, and playing.

Simultaneously, this commercial introduced Skooter, Skipper's friend. It is evident now that "friend of" meant that they could wear each other's clothes. Skooter was as ambiguous in body as Skipper, but decidedly more tomboyish. She came in assorted hair colors, in a hairstyle with two side pigtails wrapped in red bows. With her grinning face and freckles, she seemed to be a Midge equivalent. Her less refined features exaggerated her playful personality. Skooter could lead Skipper on wacky adventures. In an early color TV commercial, Skooter and Skipper are portrayed running down hills, discovering nests of baby birds in the woods. One learned that Skooter liked going to the movies and "staying to see the same picture twice, or even three times" and "turning somersaults to see the world upside down."

Skooter, Skipper's friend, also arrived in 1964, serving as a parallel to Barbie's friend Midge. This is how she looked in 1968 wearing "Patent 'N' Pants" *(above)* and carrying a miniature doll-sized Barbie doll from 1965. "School Days" *(right)* was typical of her early ensembles.

SKOOTER

A rare illustration of Barbie's family: her father, George Roberts; her mother, Margaret Roberts; her little sister, Skipper Roberts; and Barbie Roberts. Incidentally, one story divulged Barbie's middle name (Millicent) and her astrological sign (Leo). Still another mentioned that Midge had a brother, Albert.

Ricky was also ushered into Barbie's world, but who was he exactly and to whom was he related? He was an adorable little boy next door, "the cutest, freckle-faced kid in town . . . Skipper's special friend." A clue to his connection with the other dolls was provided in 1965 in the French children's magazine *Journal de Mickey*. Jouets Rationels, distributor of Mattel International's Barbie family, ran a full-page cartoon ad in the magazine showing Skooter and Ricky living in the same house. It might be presumed that they were brother and sister. However, this hypothesis cannot be proved, since this branch of the family tree was never presented in the United States. Ricky had red hair and blue eyes. His specially designed wardrobe was just right for a little boy, with names like "Lights Out," "Let's Explore," "Sunday Suit," "Little Leaguer," and "Skateboard Set."

In 1963 another doll had been born into Barbie's world, increasing the family emphasis. He was a soft vinyl baby who came with "Barbie Baby Sits." Barbie was now shown as a trustworthy teen, capable of taking charge of a small child, and thus setting an important example for doll owners. The set would change only slightly in 1965, eliminating Barbie's accessories and including more baby-sitting supplies, such as a long baby gown, cap, wrapper, formula recipe, and baby-sitter's manual. Our girl was taking on more responsibilities.

Somewhere between the appearance of Midge in 1963 and Skipper in 1964, Allan, Ken's friend, was introduced. The same body size as Ken, he had molded red hair and brown eyes, and a charming expressive face. He was, presumably, Midge's boyfriend. "He and Midge double date with Barbie and Ken," announced the booklet that at this point accompanied all the dolls and ensembles. The TV commercials elaborated on Allan's

relationship with all the members of his doll world. Janet Waldo (better known as the voice of Hanna-Barbera's Judy Jetson) explained: "Barbie is giving a surprise party in her new Dream House. . . ." The narrator confided:

. . . the guest of honor is . . . Mattel's exciting new teenage doll . . . Allan! Allan is exactly the same size as Ken, so he can wear all of Ken's handsome outfits, the way Midge wears Barbie's fabulous clothes, and Allan shares wonderful adventures with Barbie and her friends. . . . Saturday, he works at the soda fountain with Ken. And later, Allan and Midge double date with Ken and Barbie. . . . Sometimes when the weather's nice, they all go skin diving or they go on a picnic in the country. You'll love choosing outfits for Allan and Ken to go along with the ones for Barbie and Midge.

Not only were Barbie's and Ken's personalities and social life changing, but a new, more natural image was being created for them. In retrospect, Mattel designers considered the first dolls' looks too sophisticated. In 1960, Barbie's white irises were deepened to blue and her arched eyebrows were softly curved. In 1962, Ken's fuzzy hairstyle was replaced by a zippy crew cut, and his face was made narrower and more angular. Barbie and Ken were supposed to be the quintessence of wholesome activity blended with elegant and youthful physiques and high-fashion style.

The face suggests a great deal about a person. Since a doll cannot change expression, designers must consider how its face will establish the desired personality and image. As the whole Barbie idea was so new and potentially influential, Mattel was all the more challenged to portray exactly the right personalities in its plastic faces. In an article on doll making, Martha Armstrong-Hand, a designer of doll faces for Mattel from 1963 to 1981, shed some light on the subject of designing faces:

The department I joined was called Preliminary Design. In it, a group of artists worked on ideas, three-dimensional mock-ups and graphic visualization of new dolls and toys. We were a small part of the research and development group of Mattel in Hawthorne, California. For me, this was the first experience as an integrated member of a large team of product developers, for a doll at Mattel is a product. The commercial artist brings all his talent and expertise to the project. Ideas and character development as well as age, height, activity, and mechanical innards of a doll are usually determined by marketing directors, salesmen, inventors, and engineers. Some graphic input might come from the visual art department. Only then follows the dimensional birth of the doll, with face painting a second phase after sculpting. The sculptors, face painters, hair designers and costumers have to be in close touch —forming a team. Under ideal circumstances one person could do all four jobs, but with the tight schedules of a large manufacturer, specialization is more economical.

My second assignment was Midge, Barbie's girl friend. The way her eyes had been modeled made her slightly walleyed when painted. A special intense look was necessary to focus her eyes. Skipper's large eyes were difficult to focus due to the modeling. The focus of eyes can make or break a doll. About the same time, we tried to improve Barbie's makeup, but taking off her heavy eyeliner made her look too demure.

My sculpting contribution was Ricky's head. After having modeled a good-size boy's skull with a shock of hair, it turned out that the head would not pull through the little neck of Skipper's body and had to be cut down considerably. Poor Ricky! . . . Because one of our sculptors became ill, I was entrusted with a little head already roughed out by her. It became Barbie's friend, Steffie, also known as Miss America.

Skipper's friend Ricky.

Skooter visits Skipper in her "Dream Room," a classic scene of preadolescence.

One face mold modeled by a Mattel designer can serve to create several different character dolls, depending on how the face is painted, as Armstrong-Hand pointed out.

There were other changes in the dolls between 1959 and 1965. Barbie's hoop earrings had been replaced by pearls in 1960 and phased out altogether by 1965. New plastics were used to change Barbie's skin from the original dead white of 1959 to a more natural tone in the second, third, fourth, and fifth editions. Her solid plastic torso was made hollow by 1961, and the metal cylinders in her feet (like the arched eyebrows, a carry-over from *Bild* Lilli) had been eliminated completely by 1960. Saran hair replaced the older silkier hair. A new hairstyle in 1961, the famous bubble cut, also known as the beehive, was introduced soon after it was invented in Paris by Alexandre, the fabulous hairdresser. This style is perhaps the classic 1960s hairdo, and the one dearest to the hearts of Barbie owners.

The Bubble Cut Barbie came in a red maillot bathing suit and looked a lot like Suzy Parker. The doll's hair was available in variations of height, thickness, and color, which, when coordinated with different makeup, could give the impression of a number of then-popular stars and personalities, such as Sophia Loren, Elizabeth Taylor, Jane Russell, Kim Novak, and, naturally, Marilyn Monroe and Jackie Kennedy. Doll owners could also create different fantasy personalities and associations with actual family members. If, for example, your favorite aunt wore dark pink lipstick and brown eyeliner, you could conceivably find a Barbie who resembled her. Very convenient!

The wig, revived in the early 1960s, was the brainchild of Alexandre. Virtually singlehandedly, he created a zany and chic obsession for his fantasy hairstyles on both sides of the Atlantic, and the hair product and wig industry boomed. Carita in Paris, Kenneth in America, and Vidal Sassoon in London were soon to follow with startling and devastating wigs, falls, and hairpieces.

In 1963, Barbie's world commenced its own interpretation of the wig phenomenon with "Barbie Fashion Queen." "You'll love mixing and matching Barbie's costumes with her new fashion wigs," claimed the commercial. One assumes that millions of consumers *did* love mixing and matching Barbie's hairstyles. In her striped gold lamé and white strapless maillot and Cleopatra-style scarf, her introduction of wigs and hair consciousness set a precedent. From that moment on, "Glamour Goes to her Head!!"

Barbie could look like Elizabeth Taylor, Kim Novak, Marilyn Monroe—or your favorite aunt.

Fashion Queen Barbie (1963). The TV commercial for the "Barbie Fashion Queen Set" was very Hollywood. On a tremendous marquee, letters lit up one at a time, B-A-R-B-I-E, while a man's baritone voice crooned, "Barbie, you're beautiful, here's what we mean, now you've become our Fashion Queen." Then a familiar perky female voice continued, "Here's Mattel's new Fashion Queen Barbie. Now you can change her hair color and style as easily as you change her costumes. The wigs are in the latest styles—Bubble-on-Bubble, Flip, and Pageboy, in lots of different colors."

There also appeared a set called "Barbie's Teenage Fashion Model Wig Wardrobe." It included a "lovely sculptured head to put on your Barbie, then work fashion magic with three high-fashion wigs. Styles are side-part, flip, bubble-on-bubble, and pageboy. . . ." They came in the most fashionable Clairol shades of that year: "brunette, titian, and white ginger." In addition to the Ponytail Barbie, the Bubble Cut, and Wig Wardrobe, the standard Barbie had a new swept-over ponytail, known to collectors as a "Swirl."

An innovative bewigged Barbie soon appeared in 1964. Now her eyes opened and closed, and she was appropriately called "Miss Barbie." But most revolutionary were her bendable legs. Endlessly posable and more lifelike, this Barbie would mark the beginning of an era.

The Dawn of the Bendleg Era

The introduction in February 1965 of the "Barbie Look" campaign marked the beginning of a new life for the doll. With what collectors often refer to as the "bendleg era," Barbie's persona, merchandising, and fashions went through dramatic changes and became more imaginative. The new, wider oblong boxes were no longer covered with multiple drawings, but fabulous contemporary fashion photos. Realistically lit images of Barbie, Ken, Midge, Allan, and Skipper (and, in 1966, Skooter) were posed to display the bendable leg mechanism. The only text on the new boxes named the doll and mentioned its " 'Life-like' bendable legs."

The commercials on TV had a decidedly new mid-1960s ambiance, rather jazzy and "cool." A woman's voice purred, ". . . This is the newest look in fashion . . . the Barbie look! Shimmering hair in casual styles. . . . Stunning fashions, excitingly new. . . . And here's the newest thing of all —now Barbie and Midge have Mattel's special lifelike legs with knees that bend like yours!" The usual catchphrase at the end of all Mattel commercials—"You can tell it's Mattel—it's swell!"— was temporarily altered to "it's fabulous!" Over the years, it would be changed to "it's neat!", "it's mod!", and "it's groovy!" to fit the mood. These new commercials almost always showed Barbie and her family as dolls in settings of human proportion. This was in contrast to the earlier display of the dolls in little sets or with Barbie accessories, as if they were human. Frequently between 1960 and 1963, the Barbie "Dream House" was creatively used as a set for Barbie and Midge TV commercials. By 1964, however, garden walls and window ledges had become stages that offered viewers possibilities for display and play.

One of the most effective "Barbie Look" commercials at the height of this era created an explosion of pop imagery. It was a fast-talking, horn-filled, Edyie Gorme–style jazz number utilizing pop art daisies in electric pink, yellow, and green, imitating the trendy colors of London's Carnaby Street style. Flowers bounced all over the screen in the montage of a little girl, Barbie, Midge, and delightful cartoon lettering. "This is the year of the Barbie Look, and the Barbie Look is the fashion look. . . . That's right! . . . correct! . . . the swingin'est, lively'est, zingin'est fashions are the BAR-BIE LOOK!" With the clever editing and music, the action was young, fresh as paint, and very appealing.

Ken and Allan were not excluded from this zingy new attitude. The commercial assured its viewers that Ken and Allan were "really the end, so like Midge and Barbie, they're better by far,

Flirting Miss Barbie could open and close her eyes—or bat them coquettishly.

Miss Barbie appeared at the dawn of the "bendleg era" in 1965. She had "life-like bendable legs."

because they all have the look, the fashion look, the great NEW Barbie look!" Barbie's new hairstyle, called an "American girl," also a "Dutch flip," by collectors and hairdressers alike, was exactly the same as Barbra Streisand's and Liza Minnelli's that year. In 1963, Brigitte Bardot wore this style in *Paparazzi*, and may have originated it.

But the biggest hair news were Color Magic Barbie and the fabulous "Color 'N Curl" sets. "Color 'N Curl" set 4038 came with two wigs and a Barbie head similar to Fashion Queen Barbie, while set 4035 had four wigs plus a Barbie *and* a Midge head. They were remarkable, as with a special clear nonstaining solution, one could change the hair colors back and forth. The names of the colors tell the whole 1965 story: "gold" was now "lilac," "redhead" was changed to "brownie," "topaz" to "brunette," and "flame" to "carrot top." In *Vogue* that year, these shades were the predominant ones seen on models.

As for the Barbie fashions of the "bendleg era," the themes were more diverse, inspired by actual fashion trends and cultural events. Clothes showed a more imaginative variety of cuts. The 1964 Olympics in Japan initiated the travel costumes. "It's the exciting Olympic Games, and young people from all over the world are in Japan for the fun," the peppy commercial told viewers. Its ministory spoke of the adventures of Barbie, Ken, and Midge, who wore different outfits to represent different countries and participate in the fun of cultural celebrations. The dolls were "leading the grand parade . . . and the American cheering section. . . ." Sold separately were "Drum Majorette," "Cheerleader," and Ken's "Drum Major" ensemble, all nearly identical to the actual costumes worn at the Olympics.

The travel costumes took Barbie and Ken to many new places. "Barbie and Ken in Switzerland" featured Barbie in a pink skirt, a white blouse with a green bodice, an embroidered apron, an embroidered white cap, and white shoes. Of course, she carried a bouquet of edelweiss. Ken wore gray flannel shorts with red Swiss embroidery-printed suspenders, a white shirt, an alpine hat, white knee socks, and black boots. He carried a ceramic stein and a pipe. The little storybook that came with the costumes told how Ken gave Barbie the little bouquet of edelweiss and she gave him the pipe as a souvenir.

In Hawaii, Ken and Barbie were "all set to entertain at a Hawaiian luau," the booklet explained. Barbie's Hawaiian outfit included a fashionable red-and-white Hawaiian print bikini that reflected the trend of the moment to make swimsuits look Hawaiian through a bandeau effect. Barbie also had a grass skirt, a flower lei and anklet, and even a pineapple. Ken was rather seductive in a blue, green, and white print malo and a yellow lei. His straw hat was decorated with flowers, and he wore sandals and carried a ukulele.

Ken's outfit is particularly noteworthy for another reason—it seemed to contribute to more ambiguity and confusion about Ken than all his fifty conservative outfits put together. The brother of a Barbie owner recounts his terror at seeing Ken dressed in this "skirt," with his bare chest covered with flowers. He could not "figure out what was going on." In the mid-1960s, the idea of a man in a skirt was unthinkable. Presumably, Mattel initially designed this outfit as an educational device, but apparently children were not sufficiently informed to understand it.

Ken's fine, sensitive features may not have helped. The image of masculinity was changing, and Ken's naïve prepubescent looks were becoming outdated. Boyish innocence in men was no longer of social value—excitement and athletic adventure were!

Thus, in the mid-1960s Ken's image was remodeled, beginning with the names of his outfits, which were made more masculine. For example, a simple knit T-shirt and pants outfit that had been called "Casuals" in 1962 was similar to "Hiking Holiday" in 1965, with its sporty outdoor reference.

The travel costumes also included "Barbie in Mexico." The story takes the doll owner "south of the border," where "Ken wears his costume to a fiesta." Whatever questions were raised by Ken's malo were dispelled by his Mexican garb. The same man who related his insecurities about the Hawaiian "skirt" admitted that Mexican Ken was really his favorite, and he envied Ken's fancy sombrero. Finally, in homage to Japan, Mattel created "Barbie in Japan," which exquisitely portrayed her as a traditional geisha.

The "Little Theater Costume" series was equal in quality and imagination to the travel costumes. "Now you can star Barbie and Ken in your own plays," said the booklet. "They'll become romantic storybook heroes and heroines in these fabulous costumes." An orchestra tuned up in the background as the TV commercial claimed, "Backstage, you can feel the excitement 'cause it's opening night at Barbie and Ken's Little Theater! There's everything you need to put on your own shows: a curtain you can raise and lower, scripts for seven different plays, even admission tickets!"

The costumes were opulent, in rich, glittering fabrics and wonderful textures and colors. In "Barbie Arabian Nights," the dolls could portray the life of "mystery and magic in Arabia." The "Guinevere" and "King Arthur" set created "Beauty from a twelfth-century legend!" Or the dolls could portray the characters of beloved fairy tales. "Cinderella" and "The Prince" were wonderful re-creations of this romantic story. The "Red Riding Hood and the Wolf" set put Barbie in a blue-and-white dotted dress, a black corselet with gold lacing, the well-known red-hooded cape, white knee socks, and black shoes, and even in-

In the midsixties, both Barbie and Midge had wigs "for every occasion." Three wig styles—Pageboy, Flip, or Bubble Cut—accompanied Fashion Queen Barbie *(left)*. "Midge's Wig Wardrobe" offered "Swirl and Curl," which was the "American Girl" in blond; "Double Ponytail," and "Topknot Pouf," a brunet chignon with bangs and a flat black velvet bow, a look that was popular in Paris in 1964, where it was established as a classic hairstyle by Chanel.

Color Magic Barbie wearing "Color Magic Fashion Fun" (1966). Hairplay became very popular in the midsixties—for both people and dolls. Hair coloring, hair pieces, and multiple wigs were all part of high-fashion fun.

cluded a basket with rolls in a checked gingham napkin. In the drawing in the booklet, Ken was wearing only a wolf mask and the checked granny cap with his red bathing trunks and scuffs, which looked strange. Obviously, he was illustrated this way so as not to mislead customers into thinking that additional clothes came with the set. Nonetheless, he looked rather inappropriate.

The "Little Theater Gift Set" created "dramatic splendor! . . . with a wonderful theatrical wardrobe." Broadway was quite strong during the midsixties, as were the Disney versions of these classic stories. After analysis of the series and interviews with doll owners, it is clear that a child's tastes are rather unpredictable, which can be precarious for merchandising. The luxury and glamor of exotic costumes made of fantastic materials would have been stimulating to a child's imagination and probably did have educational benefits. But, alas, in spite of the tremendous appeal of the Little Theater costumes for adult collectors, the sets lasted only a year. This indicates a great deal about the level of cultural taste in American society. Children are generally accurate barometers of public taste, since they are often more honest in their reactions than are adults.

Also available for only one year, but for a different reason, were the 1964–1965 World's Fair outfits. These ensembles were designed in 1964, when the fair began, and were available only until 1965. Barbie and Skipper had coordinating outfits to wear to the fair. Skipper's "Day at the Fair" came with a remarkable miniature blond Ponytail Barbie doll in a red maillot! This was the first "doll" for the Barbie family, and is a delight to collectors. In the Tutti play set called "Let's Play Barbie," the dressed minidoll even had a miniature red Barbie case with a portrait of Bendleg Barbie on the cover. A miniature "New Dream House" for this Barbie was available with "Skipper's Dream Room" of 1965 and 1966. Theoretically, a child could go to the World's Fair with Barbie and Skipper, who could take their own Barbie dolls with them! To further this idea, Mattel created real, child-size clothing similar to the Barbie doll's outfits, with the signature print. Now a little girl could dress like the Barbie she was carrying, who was also carrying a Barbie!

Mattel even proposed a contest to win a trip to the 1965 New York World's Fair. "The grand prize is an all-expense-paid round trip for two on a luxurious TWA Starstream Jet to the New York World's Fair or to Disneyland!" exclaimed the commercial. "You can even become a member of the Barbie Fan Club if you're not a member already!" What excitement! The World's Fair was a high point of 1965, and Barbie doll owners could be involved, if only with the excitement of pretending to go to the fair with their Barbie dolls in their own backyards.

Barbie's "Dream House" reflected the suburban style that was popular in the late 1950s and early 1960s. In this scene, Color Magic Barbie, from 1966, is getting ready to split from Dullsville and take a walk on the wild side. Times changed so quickly that the busy Barbie in the background, only a couple of years older, looks like Color Magic Barbie's mom.

Not Just a Fashion Model

Barbie's world always reflected the importance of a good education. It stressed that having a balanced life of study and recreation was essential. Outfits for Barbie such as "Campus Belle" (1964–1965), "Senior Prom" (1963–1964), "Fraternity Dance" (1964–1965), and "Campus Sweetheart" (1964–1965) naturally led to "Graduation" (1963–1964). Barbie's clothes coordinated with Ken's outfits entitled "Campus Hero" (1961–1964), "Victory Dance" (1964), "College Student" (1965), and "Graduation" (1963–1964).

Barbie had a number of environments to choose from, such as "Barbie Goes to College," which came with a drive-in, dorm, malt shop, and campus. Skipper had "School Days" (1961–1966) and "School Girl" (1965–1966), which included books, pencils, a book strap, and an emblemed blazer.

It would have been tempting for the dolls to stay in school forever. But after all the proms and frat dances, these two perennial students had to make career decisions. Would Barbie become only a "Student Teacher" (1965–1966)? Or would Barbie and Ken go on to taste and select a number of challenging and dazzling careers? Barbie did have the classic Barbie ensemble, "Career Girl," in 1963 and 1964. It was a smart miniature houndstooth tweed suit à la Balenciaga. It had a straight skirt, a wide-collared portrait neckline, three-quarter sleeves, and a buttoned jacket. Under this was a red sleeveless shell. She wore a superb Mr. John–style matching cloche hat with accents of black velvet and a brilliant red rose. A pair of long black tricot gloves and a patent leather bag were the finishing touches.

In the first issue of *The World of Barbie: The Barbie Magazine Annual*, which is virtually a work of art, a poignant poem accompanies the ensemble:

The sidewalk is a magic street
Beneath our Barbie's pretty feet.
In a suit of black and white and red,
She finds fame and fortune straight ahead.

It really leaves one speechless.

Ken had ensembles such as the rare "Business Appointment" (1966), with its attaché case, leather gloves, tweed mac coat, and felt fedora hat. Also that year he wore "Summer Job." "Big Business" (1970) had flared houndstooth pants and a matching double-breasted jacket with a striped wide tie. He had a polyester business suit in 1975–1976 that matched well the "corporate" look of the 1970s.

In fact, Barbie and Ken certainly did decide to venture into many walks of life. Barbie first tried the conventional route. From the beginning, she had costumes reflecting socially acceptable goals

Barbie in "Graduation" (1963). Naturally it came with a diploma.

Barbie as "Student Teacher" (1963), with pointer and globe.

"American Airlines Stewardess"** (1961–1964) included a tailored dark blue cotton jacket and straight skirt with a crisp nylon blouse, and a pert hat with the winged insignia that matched the one worn on the jacket. Barbie also wore perfect white gloves, and carried an impeccably made replica of the famous flight bag and a black shoulder bag. In 1973, a "United Airlines Stewardess" ensemble "Friendship" came complete with serving cart, stewardess smock, and lounge table with seats for "everyone in Barbie's world."

"Busy Gal,"** a two-piece red linen suit with a red and white striped sunback blouse, blue belt, and blue shoes, came with a portfolio that held several of Barbie's fashion drawings. Even Barbie had days when she pounded the pavement looking for an elusive modeling job.

Ballerina Barbie (1976) danced on a "Ballerina Barbie Stage." Other classical costumes included "Sugar Plum Fairy," "Snowflake Fairy," and "Princess Aurora" (all 1976).

Barbie wearing "Knit Hit," a stunning two-piece knit outfit that came with flat red shoes (much to many people's surprise). It also came with a newspaper, indicating that Barbie was surely always up on the news, although in this photo she is carrying *Barbie* magazine.

Ken's doctor's outfit included a stethoscope, operating gown, reflector, surgical mask, X-rays, telephones, and towels. Barbie had a classic nurse's uniform, here modeled by her trusty friend Midge. In fact, by 1973, Barbie herself had graduated to doctor.

Ken wearing "Fun on Ice" (1963). Ken could really cut a figure, but apparently Barbie had her problems with ice skating.

for girls. The "American Airline Stewardess," introduced in 1961, was an exquisite reproduction of the actual uniform. Through the years, Barbie would wear the official costume of Pan Am, Braniff, and United Airlines. To promote the Pan Am outfit of 1966, French Mattel and Pan Am sponsored a contest in France, and the winner received an eight-day trip to the United States. In 1967, Mattel presented "Only at Ward's . . . Barbie goes Braniff," with costumes by Emilio Pucci, the famed Italian couturier. The set included a zippered boarding ensemble and the famous Pucci print head scarf with a plastic bubble helmet. Pucci's uniform for Barbie was a raspberry suit, a chic A-line dress, and "kicky" stretch culottes and top. Even the boots, shoes, underpants, and tags were perfect copies of the real Pucci-designed equivalents.

Ken was not neglected in all this globe-trotting. Available for him in 1964–1965 was "American Airlines Captain," complete with a flight log. Both airborne teens acquired a sport plane in 1964, by Irwin Corporation under license for Mattel. When mere flying wasn't enough for Barbie and Ken, "Mr." and "Miss" astronaut costumes became available in 1965, at the time when the "space race" was exciting public interest.

A more standard career choice for girls during the early sixties was nursing, and Barbie appeared as a "Candy Striper Volunteer" (1964) and a "Registered Nurse" (1961). The nurse ensemble featured a sheath uniform, a cape of blue cotton lined in red silk, a nurse's cap, and a pair of black glasses. Barbie had a medicine bottle, spoon, hot water bottle, and diploma. In the early sixties it was also appropriate for Ken to appear as "Dr. Ken." By the early seventies, Barbie would herself be a doctor, surely a direct result of the feminist movement.

By 1985, Barbie also had trained as a veterinarian, but as early as 1968 *Barbie* magazine had introduced this profession with an article entitled "If You Want to be a Veterinarian When You Grow Up." The article gave accurate and interesting information on the subject. Complementing the mood of the times, it explained that "loving animals can often give you an insight to loving your fellow man. . . ."

Barbie's interest in animals certainly might have caused her to consider being a vet. Starting with "Dogs 'N Duds" (1964), she had a gray poodle with accessories to coordinate with her clothes. Her pink, green, and white harlequin outfit and big poodle-trimmed bag came with an award certificate and trophy for her prize-winning pooch. This outfit was appropriately titled "Poodle Parade" and reflected the mid-sixties' obsession with the poodle as a snob pet and decorative motif. Today, Barbie's dog is Prince (called Lord in England). He is an Afghan, and comes with an overwhelming number of accessories.

Ken as Prince Charming, bearing a glass slipper, of course.

Barbie and Ken at the drive-in watching Barbie and Ken in *Cinderella.* Not exactly Todd-A-O, but it doesn't matter. Barbie has eyes only for her guy.

"**B**arbie in Holland" wore a traditional multistriped skirt, blue overblouse with embroidered braid trim, white apron, Dutch hat, white socks, and wooden shoes. Ken also wore a traditional costume, including white knee socks and wooden shoes. The accompanying story told how they visited Holland and decided to "go Dutch."

The "Guinevere" and "King Arthur" set outfitted Barbie in a sumptuous blue velvet gown decorated with floral braid and gold trim. She wore red armlets, red pointy brocade slippers, and a medieval-style red, blue, and gold decorated hat with a sheer fold wimple. A gold chain belt encircled her waist. Ken had an accurately styled silver lamé tunic and footed pants, over which he wore a red satin surcoat, printed with a royal-lion crest. A gold belt held his scabbard and sword. He wore red plastic spurs and carried a paper shield printed in a matching lion motif. His molded plastic helmet was an elaborate pastiche of lions and a quasi-classical border, the visor of which was permanently closed to show only Ken's eyes. Under his helmet he wore a silver lamé *cagoule*.

In honor of the 1964 Olympics in Japan, Barbie's "Drum Majorette" *(below)* as well as Ken's "Drum Major" *(opposite corner)* were designed to be nearly identical to costumes worn at the Olympics. They were accessorized with gold batons, gold-fringed epaulets, feathered busby hats, and "tennies," which was the fashionable midsixties term for sneakers.

Barbie helped Ken as much as he helped her. She was always generous and fair—although she was never a Girl Scout, as some might like to believe. A perfect modern relationship very ahead of its time.

Barbie always loved to sing, dance, and act. "I have a very lively imagination," she once said. And Ken was always there to accompany her.

Nurse Barbie escorts the ubiquitous Patty to the observation gallery to observe a heart-stopping appendectomy on her friend Billy. Patty knew that with Ken and Barbie in charge of scalpel and suture, all would be well.

Barbie as pop image
—Roy Lichtenstein,
eat your heart out!

There were numerous other dogs over the years, such as Tutti's "Me and My Dog" (1966–1968), which came with a now-rare large fluffy white dog, and "Dog Show" for Skipper featuring a white Scotty. A gray poodle came with the 1970–1971 Sears gift set called "Jamie's Furry Friends." A white dog in "Strollin' in Style" was also for Jamie. "Poodle Doodles" included a black poodle. "Hot Togs" featured a tan Afghan.

Cats were not neglected either, as "Kitty Kapers" shows, with its white Burmese. Recently, Fluff appeared as a rival to Prince, and she even had her own scratching post!

Over the years, Barbie even owned bluebirds, in "Skipper's Dream Room" (1965), and a butterfly, in Skipper's "Country Picnic" (1966), and, of course, Barbie's horses began with Dancer (1971).

Barbie had every opportunity to develop her singing career, which probably started with the "Singing in the Shower" bathtime set, to be followed by "Mood for Music" (1962–1963). Her outfit "Music Center Matinée" was a sleeveless peplumed red tunic accessorized with a silver brooch over a fashionable slim skirt. It was matched with a frosty pale tulle picture hat and long white gloves. *Parfait* for a recital. It is not surprising that Barbie, with her singing career so well developed, also possessed the complementary talent of dancing, as is reflected by the names of the clothes in her wardrobe: "Let's Dance" (1960–1962), "Dancing Doll" (1965), and "Disc Date" (1965), which came with a phonograph and a miniature Barbie hit record.

Social dance habits had changed a lot in the two decades after World War II. The lindy hop, jitterbug, and boogie-woogie steps generated further interest in wild dancing. With 1960 came Chubby Checker (né Ernest Evans), and dancing would never be the same again. Chubby Checker explained: "Before the Twist came, everyone danced together. I'm the guy that started people dancing apart. You know, I taught the world how to dance as they know it today. I'm almost like Einstein creating atomic power. Whatever dances came after the Twist, it all started here." In the July–August 1962 issue of *Barbie* magazine, one could "Join Barbie and Ken at a Twist Party," where they were "the twistingest twisters on the dance floor!" To twist, Barbie wore the perfect dress—a bell-skirted summer party dress—and Ken wore his "Saturday Date" suit.

Even though Barbie still had conservative ensembles for formal dances, with names such as "Country Club Dance," "Fraternity Dance," and "Holiday Dance" (all for 1965), most of her outfits were suited for popular dances, with names such as "The Bird," "Boogaloo," "Bristol Stomp," "The Freddie," "The Frug," "The Funky Chicken," "The Hitchhike," "The Hucklebuck" (also by Chubby Checker), and "The Hully Gully." She could be appropriately dressed to do

even the famous "Jerk" and the "Limbo," or Little Eva's "Locomotion," the "Mashed Potato," "Monkey," "Pony," "Shing-a-ling," "Slop," "Swim," and the fabulous "(Wah)Watusi." According to John and Gordon Javna in their book *60's!*, dancing in the sixties was "unstructured and easy to do—you just did whatever you wanted. . . . In fact, after a while, dancing got so wild . . . that it became a symbol of freedom. Anyone who wanted to 'let it all hang out' in public for a few hours did so on the dance floor."

But more traditional dance forms were not forgotten in the sixties. There still existed a great interest in classical dance, which for Barbie was reflected in "Ballerina" (1961–1965). Ballet and tradition would continue as an interest throughout Barbie's history with "Let's Have a Ball" (1969), "Prima Ballerina" (1970–1971), and "Ballerina Get Ups 'N Go" (1973–1974).

Barbie's dance activity even included regional dance in the "Sew-Free Fashion Fun" set entitled "Hootenanny" (1965–1966), which appeared at the same time as the popular *Andy Griffith Show*, *Petticoat Junction*, and *The Beverly Hillbillies*, all showing a revival of the "good ol' days" in response to the rapid changes of the sixties. The illustration on the box makes Barbie look like country-western legend Patsy Cline.

For the first time in a long time Ken had an opportunity to be less than classically reserved with "Ken à Go-Go." He could also dress for a "Jazz Concert" (1966) at the time when the Newport Jazz Festival was big news. There were new male singers creating a whole new style for men.

Skipper showed her enjoyment of all kinds of music when she wore an ensemble called "Platter Party" in 1965, and, of course, the quintessential "Ballet Lessons."

As the sixties exploded, Barbie kept up with the times. When the "Mod" era arrived, she was ready!

Barbie had many pets. Here is "Dogs 'N Duds" (1964), which included a few accessories just for her pet poodle.

Happiness meant belonging to the Barbie Fan Club, as is evidenced by the beaming smiles of Kim, Patty, Lisa, Cheryl, Lori, and Debby.

OFFICIAL *Barbie* FAN CLUB
MEMBERSHIP CARD
MATTEL INC. TOYMAKERS
CHAPTER # *MARGATE*
NAME *SALLY Berk*
ADDRESS *7 S Clarendon ave*
CITY *margate*
STATE *N.J.*
MEMBERSHIP # 678574
This is to certify that the above-named Barbie Fan is a member in good standing of the national Barbie Fan Club and is entitled to all rights and privileges pertaining thereto.
© 1964 MATTEL, INC.
PRINTED IN U. S. A.

Official Barbie Fan Club Membership Card (circa 1964). Sally Ann Berk of Margate, New Jersey, now a "career girl" in New York, still carries her card.

The "Barbie Goes to College" set included a drive-in, dorm, and malt shop. Here Barbie and Midge meet for gossip while Ken makes some extra bucks jerking ice cream sodas. (He was studying to be a lawyer.) Is Allan worried over a possible job interview?

Barbie Goes Mod

During the late sixties, Barbie wore an exciting array of phosphorescent, fluorescent, psychedelic print outfits. Here's Barbie gone mod in "Bermuda Holiday," a tunic dress that "traveled" with Bermuda shorts and a floppy hat. Note, too, the Herbert Levine-esque go-go boots.

Winter of 1964 saw the first U.S. television appearance of the Beatles. On the Jack Paar show of January 3, a tape of "She Loves You" was aired, followed on February 9 by the first live appearance of the Beatles on the Ed Sullivan show. There they sang "All My Lovin'," "She Loves You," and "This Boy." Their first hit, "I Want to Hold Your Hand," came out in January 1964, and suddenly the whole world was drowned in Beatlemania. In less than ten years they sold over 200 million records.

In the landmark March–April 1966 *Barbie* magazine, an article called "Where's all that Music Coming From?" inquired, ". . . what's in their music that seems to draw audiences everywhere like magic? . . . The Beatles are, of course, British, but their music comes from people of all nationalities. Have you heard their latest song? Well remember the first song they recorded . . . it's very different in melody, words and sound. That's what makes them so outstanding. Their style keeps on changing." Ken, in his mod outfit, certainly was expressing these changes.

Exciting New Friends

The swingingest new member of Barbie's family was introduced in 1966: fifteen-year-old Francie Fairchild, Barbie's "MOD'ern cousin." She was eleven and one-quarter inches tall and not as shapely as Barbie, since she was portrayed as a couple of years younger than Barbie but older than Skipper. Francie's image was almost directly inspired by "Gidget," whose real name, coincidentally, was Frances. Gidget, played by Sally Field on the TV series, was a wacky teenager who wore mod clothes, spoke hip lingo, and generally was a sensation. Barbie's cousin was introduced at the height of Gidget's popularity. She was the first doll to have rooted eyelashes. Her first edition had bendable legs; the second had the option of straight legs.

For her debut, Francie wore a polka-dot top and gingham bikini bottom—the rage at that time. (The bikini was named in France in July 1946 after the U.S. government announced that it was testing an atomic bomb near the Bikini atoll in the Pacific.) By 1966, the bomb was in the news again and so was the bikini, this time because of its popularity with women all over the world. Francie was no exception. Her bikini identified her as part of the new youth-oriented trends in fashion. Barbie, by now established with a definite personality, could not wear the kooky new styles as well as Francie could. She certainly had her share of totally mod outfits; but Francie, as she represented a new type of teen personality, could experiment with fad fashions. She could mix bell bottoms, granny gowns, miniskirts, and vinyl outfits with wild abandon.

Barbie magazine for this year painted a clear picture of the new type of teenager that emerged during the mid-sixties.

Francie, that's me—I'm Barbie's cousin (isn't she the greatest?). We have loads of fun together! She says I'm the kookiest, kickiest, most 'MOD'ern cousin a girl could ever have! That's 'cause I'm

The Fab Four.

"Ken à Go-Go" carried a flowered guitar, wore a Beatle's wig of long hair, and looked like a fashionable Londoner in a mod striped shirt and skinny pants. The illustration of Ken from the Barbie catalogue bore a striking resemblance to Paul McCartney of the Beatles.

always trying something new! Here's what I dig the very most: Rock 'n roll dances (that's me doing the frug), looooooong hair (mine comes clear down to my shoulders) and wearing all the latest teenage styles!

When Barbie comes to visit we have an absolute ball! First we make hot fudge sundaes—play all my new records. . . . Then I show her all my new clothes. . . . And my crazy patterned stockings— and my brand new granny gown! (Sometimes Barbie even lets me try on her clothes, 'cause they fit me, too.)

"Dance Party" (1966) for Francie included a record player, two Barbie records, and a hot fudge sundae with napkin and spoon, and Barbie apparently did visit, wearing "London Tour" (1966), a smart redingote of cream leatherlike vinyl complete with matching hat and bag and an aqua scarf. Little did she know what an influence her styles would really become. This outfit was a milestone marking the influence of swingin' London on Barbie's wardrobe.

By 1966, there was a whole new way of speaking. London's Carnaby Street explosion and the Beatles were partly responsible for the change in teenage lingo. The magazine included a "Say It In Mod" article to instruct: "*Mod* is short for modern and it means new. . . . *Cool* means anything that's great . . . and so does *fabby,* and *marvey* and *neat! In* means anything that's in style, *out* means anything that isn't! *Groovy* and *gear* are the same as *cool* . . . and *boss* is the very *coolest* of all. . . . So . . . if you're mod . . . that means you think Barbie and her friends are really *cool* . . . and you dig Francie because she's so *groovy* and you think you are *boss,* no matter what! Gotta *split,* now . . . See you on next month's *scene!*" This "scene" was drawn in cartoon bubbles with *Yellow Submarine*–style cartoon Edwardian-mod boys and girls as narrators.

Twist 'N Turn Francie (1969) wearing "Bridge Bit" (1967), about to play her ace in the hole.

Here's Francie, Barbie's "MOD'ern" cousin who arrived in 1966. She was as tall but not as shapely as Barbie since she was supposed to appear to be about fifteen, or a couple of years younger than her glamorous relative.

Barbie *(opposite, left)* wears a deeply vinyl expression called "Poncho Put-On." Meanwhile, Casey *(opposite, right)* goes on a fashion free-for-all with "Pazam!" an insane pink and lime vinyl coat worn over an op-art lime, pink, and yellow culotte minidress. A shocking pink braided fall and a lime-green bikini came as accessories. Francie *(near right)*, sports "Clam Diggers," an orange and yellow vinyl jacket and hat worn over orange stretch Capri pants. This outfit came with orange "girl watcher" sunglasses. Finally, Barbie *(far right)* wears "Shirt Dressy," a relatively demure afternoon dress.

In the same issue, a story, "Leave It to Francie," made a parallel between Barbie's mature yet fun behavior and Francie's vivacious and spur-of-the-moment nature. The story made it clear that Francie was fun-loving and creative. She even convinced Barbie to teach her Grandmother Rawlins to drive a "yumsville pale blue" sports car. Novel for 1966!

In 1967 several amazing things happened to Barbie, marking another new era for her family and friends. One precedent was set that year: the introduction of the first celebrity doll to Barbie's world, Twiggy. The real Twiggy (née Lesley Hornby) was a product of the mod revolution. The 91-pound, 31″-23″-32″ sprite was exactly the right look at the right time. Her skinny-as-a-twig looks were accentuated by her hair, cut in a short spiky boy's style. She spoke the same language as Francie, with a cockney twang ("It's not really wot you call a figger, is it?"). She also modeled the most *fabby* outfits to be seen anywhere at that time. Striped hip-hugger skinny pants matched a huge flowered tie and a slouchy polka-dot vest and looked terrific on Twiggy, even though they might look sloppy and in bad taste on someone else.

Schiaparelli invented the boutique, but Mary Quant was the genius behind it as we know it today. She hated straight, stuffy clothes, and in 1965 she took the street fashion of short skirts to its extreme with miniskirts. Twiggy was *the* perfect model for these clothes. She represented the new social elite "street" fashion.

The Twiggy doll had Francie's thin body and Twiggy's signature exaggerated under-eye makeup and short pale blond slicked and parted hairdo. She wore a bold-striped yellow and green mini-dress and yellow go-go boots. Twiggy was a great example of how Barbie was always active with the most important representatives of popular taste and culture.

Black or "colored" Francie was introduced in the beginning of the year. The term *colored* was soon recognized as antiquated and would be changed. However, racism was still strongly felt in America during the sixties, and moral leaders such as the Reverend Martin Luther King, Jr., and Jesse Jackson helped combat it. Godfrey Cambridge, the comedian, was, with wit and intelligence, also able to advance the civil rights cause.

The black version of Francie represented a new precedent in doll manufacturing: an already established personality doll created in two different races. It was a brilliant idea. Black Francie came dressed in a print bikini with sheer overblouse and had beautiful dark brown hair, which turned a coppery-bronze with age. However, due to the strongly established personality of the first Francie, black Francie did not sell well and was discontinued, to be replaced in 1968 quite successfully by Christie, a black doll with a personality of her very own. She had a strikingly

Mattel catalogue, 1967, featuring the real Twiggy. Managed by Justin de Villeneuve (née Nigel Davies), Twiggy was the archetypal 1960s beauty—sensual and ambiguous.

Twiggy (1967) wearing "Bloom Zoom" (1969), originally designed as a "Francie Fashion Fling." Twiggy came posed in a box as if waiting for David Bailey, England's young, upstart photographer, to snap the perfect picture.

twiggy

Posies
2/6d

TWIGGY

Here she is! Twiggy, London's top teen model, posing next to a British bus in an early ad from the Mattel catalogue: "Twiggy-Do's" (1968; *far left*) was a yellow ribbed jersey mini with stripes of green defining the hips. It was matched with the new rage—knee socks and flats—which gave an innocent-schoolgirl impression. Love beads and a shoulder-strap yellow vinyl purse were the accessories.

"Twiggy Turnouts" *(third from left)* was a sparkly multicolored mini with a wide hip-hugger silver lamé belt. Silver go-go boots could be worn with it or with the matching minibikini.

"Twigster" *(fourth from left)* took advantage of the op art obsession with a mini of orange and yellow stripes and checks and a matching fringed scarf. It came with a makeup case in orange plastic that contained eyeliner, mascara, comb, brush, mirror, and powder puff.

"Twiggy Gear" *(near left)* was a super white vinyl hip-hugger sleeveless jumpsuit with raspberry, blue, and white top and a matching floppy hat. A Hasselblad camera came with the ensemble, perfect for taking impromptu fashion snaps.

Black dolls appeared in the late 1960s. Talking Black Christie arrived in 1970 and is seen here wearing "Bridal Brocade" (1971).

Casey in her box as she looked in 1967. She had a geometric hairdo and sported one very sophisticated, very long triangular dangle earring. She wore a gold lamé hip-hugger bathing suit with a lamé fishnet jersey top and came with a coat dress and psychedelic jumpsuit.

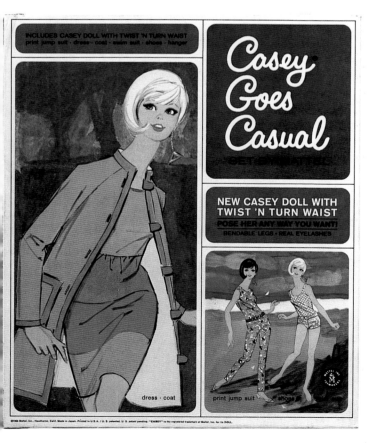

beautiful face and looked a lot like Naomi Sims, the first famous black model. Like Naomi Sims, she had a neat short "afro" hairdo, a new term for what was essentially a bubble cut. Christie would remain in the Barbie family until 1985, when Mattel would make successfully received versions of black and hispanic Barbie and Ken. Black Francie, however, was a doll that set a great precedent and remains as a reminder of political unrest during the mid-sixties.

Casey arrived on the scene in 1967 as a British friend for Francie. She was to Francie what Midge was to Barbie, a best friend, a confidante. Casey resembled the TV Gidget's friend LaRue. Theoretically, these two neato teenyboppers would be the quintessential girl friends of the era, like the girls on NBC's *Hullaballoo* and ABC's *Shindig*. Francie and Casey were as uninhibited as "the girl in the cage," frug-dancing go-go girl Lada Edmund, Jr.

Francie and Casey could hide away in Francie's house (1966), which came with not only a portable Sony-like TV, a hi-fi record player, and Italian-style plastic furniture, but a tiny typewriter so they could compose not only homework but poetry and "read-in" material. They were very much candidates for *Vogue*'s "Youthquakers" feature—with Casey posed on a stuffed leather hippopotamus sort of thing! They wore bell bottoms, granny gowns (which *Time* described as "the mumu gone MOD"), and two-tone "girl-watcher" sunglasses that looked like oodles and oodles of fun. In their miniskirts, Francie and Casey were groovy emulations of Jean Shrimpton's persona.

Nineteen sixty-seven was a pretty extraordinary year for Barbie herself. Ken left the scene. Whether he hitchhiked to Haight-Ashbury or to Canada, or just went off to grow his hair, he left Barbie to fend for herself. Midge was discontinued, too. Some say she got married (Allan was also suspiciously missing), as evidenced in a 1964 FAO Schwarz Children's World Christmas catalogue item, "Midge and her Trousseau." (True to form, "Midge and her Trousseau" came with a wedding gown, a blue garter, a garden party dress, cocktail dress, glasses, jewelry, purses, hats, shoes . . . and a telephone to call her mom—just in case!)

Midge had even moved out of the "Barbie and Midge Wardrobe Case" and into her own "Midge, Barbie's Best Friend" case. Gone were the days when Barbie and Midge would star in TV commercials that boasted of how the fashions they wore would suit a "teenage fashion model and her best friend." In the far past were the ensembles such as "Pajama Party," where she wore "tailored but dainty pale blue pajamas for that late-nite gab-fest with Barbie!" and could be awakened "by her own alarm clock in time for important fashion model assignments." She did have fond memories of her own "Ensemble Gift Set" in 1964. Wasn't she also in several "Barbie and her Friends" gift sets? Wasn't she a *genuine* Midge?

Stacey, Barbie's English friend, arrived in 1968. Here she is wearing "All That Jazz," a low-belted coat dress that came with matching sparkle hose.

"Hey Wow! P.J.'s here!" the TV ad exclaimed when P.J. arrived in 1969. Here she is wearing a pastel knitted micromini and "Love Beads" in her hair. But *wait*! Isn't there something familiar here? Yes! In fact, P.J. is Midge reincarnate! She was made with Midge's headmold.

Ken disappeared in 1967 (with Midge, perhaps?) but returned, true blue, looking like a real "guruvy" guy. Here he is, circa 1969, wearing "Suede Scene" (1972).

Here's Skipper wearing "Fancy Pants" (1969), which came with a pink vinyl bag to match the pink vinyl bodice.

Good old Midge, as she looked when she left Hawthorne in 1967. While Barbie was going funky and mod, Midge appeared a little square. Here she is in "Suburban Shopper," one of Barbie's old faves from 1959, with its cute cartwheel hat and fruit-filled tote bag. This outfit came with a sweet necklace and a telephone. Midge must have felt that once she moved to the Boonies she'd have to phone in for the latest fashions.

Bendleg Twist 'N Turn Casey (1967) wearing "Culotte-Wot?" (1968), an A-line miniculotte in shocking pink with white satin bow and pockets. It came with white fishnet hose, pink knee-high boots, a white satin floppy hat, and lime-green goggles with pink polka dots. She also had such outfits as "Ten-terrific" emulating a typical John Bates look, and "The Silver Cage," a Paco Rabanne-style dress.

Midge was definitely genuine, as her tag claimed. But doll owners remember Midge as the one assigned the drearier outfits such as "Fancy Free" (1963–64), a plainish cotton dress trimmed with old-fashioned rickrack, or "Orange Blossom" (1961–1964). Midge was always the bridesmaid, never the bride. Not for her the glamorous frothy gowns or the exciting sports clothes, although the illustrations in the booklets alternated between Barbie and Midge. Owners do, however, remember her new hairdo when bendlegs were introduced, and her neat aqua striped swimsuit, and, of course, her freckles!

Nobody could really dislike Midge, the same way nobody could really dislike Cathy Lane, Patty Lane's cousin on the *Patty Duke Show*, or, for that matter, Ethel Mertz or Betty Rubble. Midge simply let her contract run out and didn't return to the sacred domain of Mattel in Hawthorne to renew it. She left her origins and drove to Los Angeles. As she looked up at the Hollywood Hills sign, she knew it would be perhaps for the last time. She drove on, out of California, away from the glamor of being the best friend of the world's most famous teenage fashion model doll, away from the stunning pink-striped boxes of to-the-minute fashion ensembles, pak items, and exclusive Mattel fashions. She drove away from days of several different hair colors. She just drove out into Middle America. The only reminder of Midge was a dusty old "Barbie Family 'N Friends Tree" in a 1968 *Barbie* magazine.

With Ken, Allan, and Midge gone, Barbie was all alone. Skipper, Tutti, and Todd (her tiny sister and brother, introduced in early 1966) and their tiny friend Chris needed looking after. Francie and her best friend Casey were off being groovy together. They could take care of themselves. What's a Barbie doll to do? With a stiff upper lip, in the true Barbie manner, she did the only thing any fabulous teenage fashion model doll could do —she updated her look and persona.

The Twist 'N Turn Era

The "Twist 'N Turn era," beginning in 1967, marked another departure for our heroine. Barbie could now twist to accommodate all the swinging new dances that required pivoting at the waist. Highly significant! She had long eyelashes, just like her cousin, paler skin, bendable legs, and a super new FACE! Yes, Barbie's whole face changed to better represent the contemporary teenager. Her face was now younger, more wide-eyed, more innocent, and much less sultry. Her hair, which was completely straight and a little longer than shoulder length, came in the style of the newly famous folk singer Joan Baez. It looked as if it had been ironed between brown paper bags, as teenagers did at that time to straighten curly hair. Barbie's hair colors were named "Summer Sand," "Chocolate Bon-Bon," "Cupa-Co-Co," and "Sun Kissed." Straight bangs and pulled-back sides were accentuated by a little orange bow on top. This new Barbie wore an orange bikini under a sleeveless step-in white mesh suit, terrifically nostalgic of Annette Funicello's 1965 swimsuit in the film *Beach Blanket Bingo*. Funicello's suit was designed to hide her navel, something that her Disney contract insisted upon. It was probably conceived at the time of the famous "Scandal Suit" by Cole of California—a regular maillot with a mesh inset exposing a little cleavage.

The first TV commercial showing this new Barbie featured a jubilant Maureen McCormick of *Brady Bunch* fame, who posed the poignant question: "But what do I do with my old Barbie doll?" The answer was: children could actually trade in their old Barbies, and for a dollar and fifty cents buy this new, improved one. Very clever! In May alone, 1.2 million dolls were turned in, which eventually were given to charity.

The question arises, can one take an already established personality with a strong visual image and drastically change that image, yet still retain the doll's popularity? Certainly! The eight years between the first *haute couture* Barbie and the new "Barbie à la love beads" saw irreversible changes. By 1967, ten-year-old girls who were anxious to be groovy wrote poems about being free and conjured up Peter Max images. It was the year of "Incense and Peppermint" by the Strawberry Alarm Clock. This new audience was ready to exchange the heavy eyeliner, the pageboy, the once-adored bubble cut and arched eyebrows of the old Barbie for a more trendy look. The trade-in campaign was a brilliant idea to introduce a new Barbie aesthetic and allow it to instantly infiltrate the secret Barbie living quarters cached in every little girl's night table and playroom toy shelf.

In the late 1960s, the culture that produced paper dresses, instant soup, and inflatable furniture could only applaud the transformation of the world's leading fashion doll. A butterfly she was. Twist 'N Turn Barbie was introduced in a commercial that masterfully reflected the times. Dozens of little girls of different races, all wearing basically the same affluent American outfit, skipped about, clutching the démodé Bubble Cut Barbie. They entered a cartoon-style toy store, where they each received a new Twist 'N Turn Barbie from a robotic Geppetto-like cartoon salesman. The scene was decorated with huge pop art daisies and a smiling sun. A second commercial posed the vital question: "What is your Barbie like?" Does she like the theater? Walks in the park? Sports? The same fabulous fantasy of teenage life existed with this new Barbie.

TWiST 'N
TURN

Twist 'N Turn Barbie (1969) wearing "Fancy Dancy" (1969). This was the famous promotional Barbie.

In 1970, author Alvin Toffler offered another view of the radical change in Barbie's life in his controversial book *Future Shock*. In a chapter entitled "Things: The Throw-Away Society," Toffler discussed the trade-in campaign:

What Mattel did not announce was that by trading in her old doll for a technologically improved model, the little girl of today, citizen of tomorrow's super-industrial world, would learn a fundamental lesson about the new society: that man's relationships with things are increasingly temporary. . . . Anti-materialists tend to deride the importance of 'things.' Yet things are highly significant not merely because of their functional utility, but also because of their psychological impact. We develop relationships with things. Things affect our sense of continuity. . . . or discontinuity. They play a role in the structure of situations, and the foreshortening of our relationships with things accelerates the pace of life. Moreover, our attitudes towards things reflect basic value judgments. Nothing could be more dramatic than the difference between the new breed of little girls who cheerfully turn in their Barbies for the new improved model and those who, like their mothers and grandmothers before them, clutch lingeringly and lovingly to the same doll until it disintegrates from sheer age. In this difference lies the contrast between past and future, between societies based on permanence, and the new fast-forming society based on transience . . . . This child soon learns that Barbie dolls are by no means the only physical objects that pass into and out of her young life at a rapid clip.

Alas, to thing or not to thing. Toffler's now-dated observations did not anticipate the recognition and glorification of Barbie—old and new—by the new generation of little girls and adults alike. He could not fit into his thesis the fact that Barbie would be hailed as a great symbol, or that she would be collected and valued as an important icon of her society. The meaning of the trade-in was not that one merely surrendered a possession to Big Brother. Like her predecessor, the new Barbie continued to fulfill the creative needs of children. Trading in the old Barbie was as harmless as a trip to the hairdresser.

With the trade-in campaign, Barbie merrily went on her way with her usual panache, and the transition to the mod era was now complete. In 1965 and 1966, fashion still dictated classic *haute couture*–looking ensembles such as the Sew Free outfit "Moonlight and Roses," or outfits such as "Debutante Ball" and "Pretty as a Picture," but by 1967, Barbie's clothes were transformed into costumes such as "Color Magic," "Pretty Wild," a drop-waist pop and op-art print with matching satchel and floppy hat, or "Sun Flower," a mini–shift dress with huge pop plastic purple and pink dangle earrings. The see-through look was inter-

Barbie and her friends wore a host of op, pop, and print outfits during the sixties. They had names like "Fur Out," "Go Granny Go," "Drizzle Dash," "Mini-Prints," and "Disco Dater." Shown here are "Style Setters" *(below)*, a wild colored sheath with matching hose, velvet cape, and hood; "Trailblazers" *(top right)*, a corduroy striped pantsuit with coordinating polka-dotted sunglasses; and "Bouncy Flouncy" *(bottom right)*, which came with a matching tote.

preted in "Jump into Lace," a sleeveless white lace jumpsuit, and also clear mod boots in the style of Herbert Levine. Courrèges' influence was obvious in ensembles such as "Zokko!" in silver and blue Mylar with Courrèges-style boots, and "Snap-Dash," a green mini trimmed in vinyl with a stylized western hat.

Even Barbie's "Family House" was a tribute to the new Carnaby Street psychedelic cartoon colors —a big contrast to her previous ranch-style suburban house. More like an apartment than a house, it had a built-in bucket sofa and Danish fireplace.

Similar to the "Barbie Wig Wardrobe" of 1964, there was a new "Barbie Hair Fair," which came with a Barbie head with a new face and a short hairdo à la Joey Heatherton, possibly invented to prevent children from cutting Barbie's long hair. (One often comes across old Barbie dolls with hacked Sassoon bobs, no doubt the work of their young barbers!) The 1969 "Hair Fair" set included a dark wig similar to Marlo Thomas's hairdo on *That Girl*, her hit TV show. This coiffure would become the official hairstyle of the second-edition Twist 'N Turn Barbie of February 1969.

The year 1968 came in with yet another blast. *Talking Barbie!* Big, big news! The last time we actually heard Barbie's voice was way back in 1961, when singer Charlotte Austin provided the voice on the "Barbie Sings" record and on the Barbie Mattel-a-Phone. Now, Barbie said incredible things in both English and Spanish. Her two fabulous new friends, British Stacey and Christie, could talk too. They said such typical teenage things as "I think miniskirts are smashing!" (that from British Stacey) and Barbie's "Should I change my hairstyle?"

By 1968, Barbie, now a full-fledged chanteuse, was wearing Biba-style clothes such as "All That Jazz." "Festival Fashion," with its reference to Woodstock, was a wild pair of balloon pants in a flower print with a fringed belt, pink vest, ruffled balloon-sleeved blouse, and pink bandana head scarf. "Groovin' Gauchos" acknowledged the popular gaucho pants seen at the time on fashion mannequins such as Penelope Tree and Marisa Berenson. Psychedelic prints made these clothes "groovin'." The accompanying fashion record, "Rapping in Rhythm," rhapsodized "loving your brother, loving one another," in true sixties style.

In spite of all this freewheeling fun, the emphasis in the 1968 *Barbie* magazine was on school and school clothes. "It's been a great summer, full of swimming, parties, and get-acquainted chats for the three popular teenagers. But now, the girls are ready to put away their swimsuits because school is here, and so are their back-to-school wardrobes. And since Barbie's new friends are the same size she is, they have all sorts of wild accessories to share, like sandals, mesh stockings, chain

In the midsixties, Barbie got a new hairstyle called "American Girl," also known as a "Flip." Barbra Streisand, Liza Minnelli, Marlo Thomas, and hosts of American teens adopted the look.

Long straight hair was the rage in the midsixties. Little girls—and not-so-little girls—would go to "great lengths" to relinquish those curls.

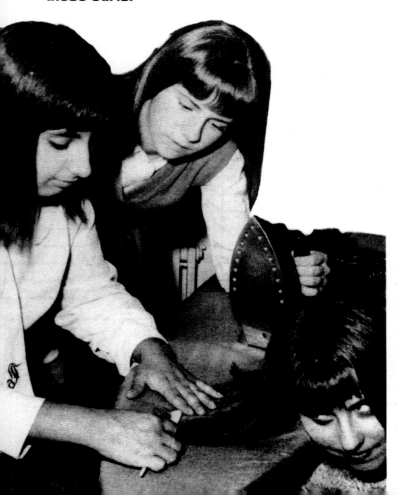

belts, capes, and even fashion's newest idea: the tunic. . . ." Barbie even had a princess phone to talk on, perhaps to enable her to tell everyone about her newest outfits, "Now Wow" and "Twinkle Togs," in neon Mylar fabric. Rudi Gernreich's colorful twenties'-style space cadet clothes were the influence behind Barbie's "Scene Stealers" outfit, a confection of glittery sheer nylon used to create a "kiss and blush" pink minicoat piped in green satin over a lime lamé blouse and sheer pink ruffled mini trimmed in lime. There was nothing too wild, too daring, or too pink for Barbie and her friends.

The new dolls certainly had a lot to talk about. Nineteen sixty-eight was the year of "Hello, I Love You" by the Doors, "Mellow Yellow" by Donovan, "Hey Jude" by the Beatles, "Love Child" by Diana Ross and the Supremes, and "Judy in Disguise (with Glasses)" by John Fred and his Playboy Band. Tiny Tim was clutching daisies on the cover of *Rolling Stone*. Rowan and Martin's *Laugh-In* was shocking America as one of its stars, Judy Carne, shimmied, nearly nude and painted with "Sock It to Me." The Campbell kids wore Nehru jackets and love beads in a garden of flowers. Pepsi was pouring it on as the world wore paper dresses printed with Apollo moon rockets and Allen Ginsberg poems. Pants were still considered unladylike, but they appeared in Italian and French *haute couture* and in Barbie's closet. Expressions that Barbie probably heard were "tune in," "turn on," "rap," "good vibes," "spaced out," "outta sight," "far out," "flipped out," "blow your mind," "power to the people," "uptight," and "right on."

The drug culture and the artistic temperament dictated the new world aesthetics. Geometric op art became mixed with flowing art nouveau images. "Barbie's New Family House" sported a Carnaby Street sign and a black-and-white op art entry hall and flowery art nouveau woman's portrait. Clothing reflected perfectly the new mood. Romantic, layered, ruffled mini outfits were turning into semiethnic outfits with wild beaded earrings that brushed the shoulders. Designers such as Giorgio Sant'Angelo were painting Twiggy and Veruschka with flowers and twisting them up in pastiches of 1890-style "flower power" and Day-Glow African prints. Barbie even wore ensembles emulating the Paris high-fashion craze for Courrèges, Cardin, and Saint Laurent. Paraphernalia, the store that carried Betsey Johnson's stretchy Chelsea Girl style clothes, would have been the perfect place for Barbie to shop, as well as the most dazzling store in the world. Biba in London, the creation of Barbara Hulanicki, Mrs. Leonard Holzer, Baby Jane to her *intimes*, probably had similar taste in boots to Barbie. In *Vogue*, Baby Jane was photographed wearing a minicoat of cheetah trimmed in lynx with matching "long, long, long boots."

New Talking Barbie (1967) wore a shocking-pink micromini with yellow trim and pink briefs. Her hair was side plaited with elaborate pink ribbon bows running through it and groovy spit curls on the side. Owners could choose hair colors like "Chocolate Bon-Bon," "Sunkissed," or "Cupa-Co-Co."

The illustration on New Talking Barbie's box shows her wearing "Dinner Dazzle," a relatively conservative ensemble.

NEW TALKING
Barbie

Dinner
Dazzle
Set
BY MATTEL

Complete with
Talking Barbie Doll!
She says many things!
You never know
what she'll say next!
Pull Talking Ring
on back of box!

INCLUDES TALKING BARBIE DOLL WITH BENDABLE LEGS, REAL EYELASHES,
SWIMSUIT, JACKET WITH 'FURRY' COLLAR, SKIRT, BLOUSE, HOSE, SHOES.

I TALK!

NEW!
TALKING
Barbie®
BY MATTEL

©1967 Mattel, Inc. Printed in U.S.A.

Mrs. Leonard Holzer (Baby Jane to her friends) shared Barbie's taste in long, long, long boots.

Edie Sedgwick, one of the greatest symbols of the 1960s, was first seen in *Vogue* in 1965 in a column called "Youthquakers." She was described as "twenty-two, white-haired with anthracite-black eyes and legs to swoon over." She once appeared at Chez Castel in Paris with Andy Warhol and fifteen rabbits "in a black leotard and white mink coat. In her deep, campy voice, strained through smoke and Boston, she said: 'It's all I have to wear.' "

Nineteen sixty-nine was the year to "Let Yourself Go," announced *Vogue*, and Barbie's world was "Bright, Swingin', Now!" To accommodate the new types of images that youth portrayed, Mattel introduced Stacey, Barbie's British pal, in 1968 and P.J., Barbie's "new and groovy" friend, in 1969. P.J. talked in the newest lingo, saying things like "Wow! You're the grooviest!" One can imagine how Midge might have felt when she was introduced—it was all so new and thrilling. When she left, some say, she sensed the changing times and had a premonition about Stacey and P.J. Who knows? It was true that Stacey was more "with it" than Barbie's first friend. Now there was P.J., perhaps even more "with it" than Stacey. But *wait.* Don't we recognize that face? Why yes! P.J. was made with Midge's head mold. Midge had returned, combed out her flip, and dyed it platinum! With a bit of makeup and some new threads, she was the delicious new alias, P.J. Yet when girls wrote Mattel, asking "What does P.J. stand for?" they received the answer: "Nothing."

Midge couldn't let Barbie down; after all, she was her best friend. In fact, years later it was discovered that she was really Barbie's cousin! A Toys R Us special gift set that included P.J. announced the family ties. So blood, in this case, was thicker than water, and loyal Midge in the guise of P.J.

returned to Barbie's world. Needless to say, Barbie was thrilled.

P.J. debuted in an orange and pink mod flower print micromini with flared hem and bell sleeves. Underneath, she wore the current rage, pink lace-trimmed panties. She had two side ponytails wrapped in the Indian love beads that everyone was stringing at the time. She wore the currently popular rose-colored bubble glasses and the newly fashionable chunky-heeled shoes. Nearly immediately there was a Twist 'N Turn P.J. gift set for Sears and marvelous pak items with love beads, chain necklaces, and a zingy assortment of vinyl boots to appeal to P.J.'s taste. Mattel's *Barbie Talk* magazine allowed the two old friends to catch up on lots of stories and adventures.

In spite of all the cheery fun and giddy enthusiasm, Barbie needed a boyfriend, so Mattel brought back Ken in 1969 after a two-year absence. He was not the Ken we used to know, however, but a completely "New, good-lookin' Ken, all 'round guy. . . ." He was "huskier and more handsome than ever." He spoke in a baritone in English or Spanish. Ken's new voice sounded different from that of Bill Cunningham, the original Ken on the 1961 "Barbie Sings" record. Early Ken had a rather collegiate Ricky Nelson voice. Now he sounded more mature, although he had lost none of his enthusiasm for Barbie. It was as if he'd never been gone.

What had he done while he was away? He was no longer like Dwayne Hickman and Tony Dow but more like Warren Beatty, Peter Fonda, or Clint Eastwood in looks. His longer brown hair was in an Edwardian-style side part with a fringe that swept across his forehead. His face had a cool, debonair look that was very Sean Connery. The illustration on the booklet that accompanied him even showed Barbie wielding a gold pistol. Now, with Ken so cool, they could be the new *Avengers* couple, with Barbie as Emma Peel.

Ken's outfits complemented his new macho persona, as his new muscular body could no longer fit into his old wardrobe of collegiate clothes and theater costumes. His new sense of dressing was reflected in his four basic outfits. "Breakfast at Seven" was a pajama and robe set in a yellow and orange grid pattern; it came with an electric razor. "Rally Gear" was a Steve McQueen–style double-breasted leather racing jacket with a madras striped shirt and skinny gold jeans. Ken wore them with brown "leather" cowboy boots. "Town Turtle" was a wide-lapeled, double-breasted sports jacket with checked bell bottoms and a white turtleneck pullover. His "Guruvy Formal" featured white linen pants worn with a red taffeta Nehru jacket, under which was a Donovan-type Nehru shirt with bell sleeves and a glittering red and gold brocade vest. He wore a silk and gold lamé ascot. This was the perfect outfit for Ken to accompany Barbie when she wore "Yellow Mellow," a simple velvet miniskirt.

Sears Exclusive "Red, White, and Wild" had the quintessential polka dot wide-tie and flared blazer which was double-breasted and striped.

It was a strategic year, before "hip" became "hippie." The illustrations on the gift sets of this period were in the then-popular Leroy Neiman style, with the glamorous twilight look and grainy painted backgrounds. This style was effective on gift sets such as "Dinner Dazzle Set" (1967), "Travel in Style Set" (1967), "Beautiful Blues Set," and the "Stripes Are Happening" set (1968) for Stacey.

In addition to greeting her old friends, Barbie welcomed with great pleasure two new celebrity dolls: Truly Scrumptious from the film *Chitty, Chitty, Bang, Bang* and Julia of NBC's hit TV program starring Diahann Carroll, the first black actress to star in her own comedy series. She portrayed an independent woman, widowed when her husband was killed in Vietnam. The show's stories were based on her home and office life and were all racially integrated. Julia by Mattel had four outfits just for her, the way Twiggy wore her own special looks.

As always, Barbie and her friends personified the best in current fashion and current customs. When the seventies arrived, Barbie was ready again to move with the times. And move she did!

A *T.V. Guide* ad for Barbie promoting the fact that "now the most famous fashion doll can talk! So can her friend Stacey," who spoke with an English accent.

Now Look Ken (who didn't look particularly "now" until 1976) wearing a hippy-dippy psychedelic pantsuit (circa 1969). The expression "Hippy," part of "Hippy-Dippy," is thought to have been the sarcastic catch-phrase of San Francisco columnist Herb Caen, and was originally considered to be another device the media used to avoid having to deal with someone as an individual.

Talking Busy Barbie (1972) in her original outfit, a pair of shiny (and controversial) hot pants with detachable bib, a red turtleneck sweater, and matching red headband. She is holding with her "clasping hands" her very own portable TV.

Barbie Twists, Turns, Jumps ...and Goes!

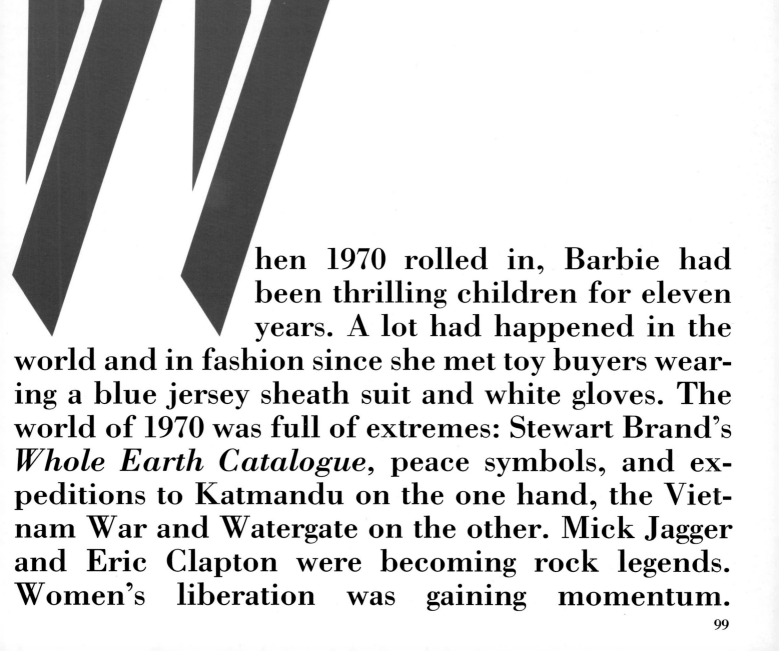

hen 1970 rolled in, Barbie had been thrilling children for eleven years. A lot had happened in the world and in fashion since she met toy buyers wearing a blue jersey sheath suit and white gloves. The world of 1970 was full of extremes: Stewart Brand's *Whole Earth Catalogue*, peace symbols, and expeditions to Katmandu on the one hand, the Vietnam War and Watergate on the other. Mick Jagger and Eric Clapton were becoming rock legends. Women's liberation was gaining momentum.

Expressions like "try to relate" and "what a gas" held great meaning for those who used them.

In fashion, all was its usual hectic, contradictory, exciting self. Sexy was in! Health and naturalness were stressed, yet every type of gadget, fad, and fashion was available in boutiques with names like "Mr. Freedom" and "Granny Takes a Trip." Youth became known as hippies. Brotherhood, unwed motherhood, love-ins, meditation, transcendental Timothy Leary, and politicizing Abbie Hoffman were all heard from, along with talk about communes.

Fashion in 1970 looked unusual, to say the least. Paris and Italian couture showed marvelous things based on what hippies were inventing, and the people who were not quite hippies adored these clothes, finding them uninhibited. Socialites in Paris, New York, London, Milan, and Los Angeles thought it was fabulous to wear patchwork, crocheted belts and hats, American Indian jewelry, and layered peasant costumes, along with distressed leather belts covered in grommets and studs. Rings on every finger, head scarves, and thongs that laced up the leg, when artistically pulled together by the likes of Giorgio Sant'Angelo, were exotic and vibrating with all the music and freedom of those naïve times.

It was the beginning of bra burning and the end of the era when designers dictated hemlines and styles. Fashion was considered by some as fine art, or vice versa. Everything was starting to blend and blur into new, unheard of associations. When singer Janis Joplin had her T-shirts and satin sheets tie-dyed, they appeared in American *Vogue*. Ara Gallant was considered a genius for what appeared to be messing up Lauren Hutton's hair on the cover of that same magazine. Paco Rabanne showed his clothing at modern art museums, and Ungaro was among the first to display body sculpture by Oscar Gustin with his couture. Soon artists were making elaborate harnesses of metal and leather that would be seen all over *Vogue*'s pages. That always-enthusiastic fashion interpreter, in its January 1, 1970, issue, had the following to say about the new decade:

> *It's a new Decade*
> *A whole new Ballgame*
> *Are You Ready for it?*

It took the sixties to knock old standards of beauty into a cocked hat and change the very meaning of fashion—it was just that mix of inventiveness and recklessness we needed to escape the cookie-cutter mold and see that fashion today is simply how attractively and comfortably we make ourselves heard in what Baudelaire called the Great Parade of Modern Life. . . . Today's Triumph is the vitality and imagination of those who live the life well. They—and never again the fashion dictators—will lead the whole roiling, moiling, magical Parade right up to the 'seven-ties, and pull everyone along with them to still greener fields of opportunity.

Mattel, in 1970, its twenty-fifth-anniversary year, was no exception to this social climate of extreme optimism. At that time, Elliot Handler, founding member and chairman of the board, wrote: "Each of our twenty-four years has been an exciting and challenging one. This, our twenty-fifth, is both a milestone in growth and progress and a springboard to the next quarter century." Nineteen seventy, in spite of a fire that destroyed a Mattel factory in Mexico, would see an incredible new Barbie that would represent this new freedom. Dramatic New Living Barbie was the most posable Barbie doll ever made. She swiveled at the waist, neck, hands, and legs. She was bendable in natural ways at the elbows, knees, ankles, and wrists. Her head tilted beguilingly. Her arms swung around. "As posable as you are," claimed the advertising. Her hairstyle was casual and a bit like champion skier Suzy Chaffee's; shoulder length with bangs, it came in the usual choice of colors. Barbie had thick, long eyelashes. This Barbie was in movability miles away from that first Barbie, who could only move her legs at the hips and her arms at the shoulders. Naturally, with the new doll, all the emphasis was on movement.

Dancing, jumping, playing, and embracing the world, the women of 1970 were seen flying across the pages of fashion and sports magazines in mid-air photographs. Fashion photographers such as Gianni Penati, Patrick Litchfield, Richard Avedon, and Bert Stern captured the jump-for-joy attitude of these times. Dramatic Living Barbie was posed and photographed in the very same manner. In the first TV commercial for this doll, Maureen McCormick ran, jumped, and twirled around a Barbie posed as she was.

MATTEL 1970 Dolls
Our 25th Year

Spring

Living Barbie (1970) wearing "Shape-Ups" (1970).

A Mattel catalogue from 1970 featuring "New! Dramatic! Living Barbie" who had arrived in 1969 but was already a seventies girl . . . pert, perky, and totally posable. "It makes playing Barbie a whole new thing," the TV ads announced.

Barbie and her pals evolve from the sixties into the seventies.

Barbie wearing "Lemon Kick," a Mary McFadden-esque pantsuit, circa 1970.

Fringe, fringe, fringe. Live Action P.J. goes berserk.

Barbie now wore a two-tone Mylar one-piece swimsuit with a hooded jacket in net. The emphasis on her posability and the new cultural emphasis on health and sports (which would be the whole thrust of the decade) made it evident that she would have a lot of sports-oriented ensembles in the years to come. While in 1965 all she had was a book on *How to Lose Weight* that came with her "Slumber Party" set, in 1970 she could wear "Shape-Ups," an outfit that included red panty hose, a leotard, dumbbells, an exercise book, a rope, and a body toner called "Mattel's Twister." Instead of wearing her original "Open Toe Springolator" high heels, Barbie could now sport sensible red flats, thanks to her bendable ankles. She could also step up on her bathroom scale to discover happily she weighed only 110 pounds.

As the fashions of the seventies rolled out, Barbie picked up on each one's momentary chic. "Fringe, Fringe, Fringe . . . on shawls, as trim, on everything," cried *Women's Wear Daily*, and Barbie had her share on the brightly colored shawl in "Rainbow Wraps" and on the hem of "Fiery Felt." She wore ethnic looks with "Gypsy Spirit," a vested aqua felt outfit with skirt trimmed in gold thread and pink and green yarn crochet. She reflected Mary McFadden's Fortuny style in "Lemon Kick," a pleated tunic pantsuit, now finally acceptable as an alternative to dresses. Palazzo pants and the lamé brocade craze found comfortable and enthusiastic interpretation in "Firelights" and "Bright 'N Brocade." Francie wore "Long on Leather," a red vinyl maxi with fringed scarf. Snake and lizard prints, the veritable rage of the early seventies, were seen in Francie's "Snake Charmers." Animal prints were featured in "Pony Coat" for Francie and "Leisure Leopard" for Barbie, a jumpsuit.

The ultimate fashion of 1970 was the maxicoat. Barbie had the incredible "Maxi 'N Mini," a very Anita Pallenberg style with its hip-length Mylar high-heeled boots and Lurex striped miniskirt under a blue-trimmed Mylar maxi. Perfect for a rock 'n' roll date at Max's Kansas City. Halston's slinky jersey clothes had their influence very quickly in fashion, and soon Barbie was wearing "Shift into Knit," a simple shift with a fringed scarf. Francie had a soft jersey outfit in red and blue called "Striped Types." Denim would become à la mode, along with headbands, platform shoes, suede shoulder bags, and retro 1920s and 1940s styles.

The "romantic era" in the world of Barbie had just begun. Even Tutti had a hippie outfit complete with love beads, bell bottoms, and a fringe suede vest for the "Grobe Ferien" doll from Germany.

Nineteen seventy also saw new friends for Barbie. Talking Brad was the first black male friend in her world. He was the same size as Ken and had a handsome face with molded hair in a short afro

Scott, Skipper's boyfriend, arrived in 1980. Here he is on his way to the boardwalk in Venice, California.

style. The packaging for Ken's outfits now included Brad's name, and together they modeled the new outfits.

Menswear in general was making a big transition to more relaxed styles. *Unisex* was just being coined, and psychedelia was actually marketed for men. Ken had shirts with op art prints. Even his shoes were cool slip-on loafers, which were making news in Italian menswear circles and were interpreted as the "Monkee Boot" by Thom McAn. No one could accuse the new Ken or Christie's boyfriend Brad of being "uptight."

Walking Jamie was a Sears exclusive. She had a demure new face and flip hairstyle tied with a head scarf of purple chiffon. She wore a yellow turtleneck op print mini. A button panel on her back made her legs move and gave the impression that she really walked.

With the advent of frivolous clothes and fabulous friends to party with, hairdos became froufrou and once again an obsession. Alexandre was making superb wigs in bright colors for Courrèges, and models were just starting to dye parts of their hair blue and pink. Ara Gallant was creating veritable artworks on famous models' heads using their own hair. Hairdressers were idolized as stars. *Shampoo*, a movie about the exploits of a superstar cum hairdresser, exemplified this trend. So this new decade of Barbie opened with "Francie's Hair Happenin's," which came with four wigs and a Francie doll with "Growin' Pretty Hair" that, through an inner mechanism, really seemed to grow longer. Francie was, of course, dressed in wonderfully mod mini outfits. Later in 1971, there would be Barbie doll versions with growing hair also.

Also in 1971 came the "Live Action" dolls and the "Malibu" series. The Malibu dolls reflected the easygoing, tan, California lifestyle. Being the first actual suntan dolls, they came dressed in light-colored bathing clothes, with sunstreaked hair and pleasant smiles. The Malibu dolls provided an alternative to the wilder side of Barbie's culture, and they also proposed extended play with a number of exciting accessories.

"Sun 'N Fun Buggy" was a dune buggy covered in "Love Bug" style daisy decals. The "Barbie Country Camper" was "a home for Barbie wherever she explores the great outdoors. . . . The swingin'est camper on wheels." The commercial, sung in country-and-western style, claimed that "the road never ends in Barbie's New Country Camper." Included were many camping basics such as sleeping bags, stools, and a fold-out tent. The camper was of sturdy orange, pink, and yellow plastic that could be used for millions of Barbie-size adventures. Ken had a "Surf's Up" gift set that included a "Skim Board" to ride the waves. Francie could also surf while wearing her 1973 beach outfit.

As a matter of fact, although these sporty,

Malibu Christie wearing "Sears Regulation Olympic Outfit" (1976). There were many official U.S. Olympic outfits and accessories for Barbie and her friends, available from Sears.

Free Moving Curtis (1974) wearing "Big Business" (1972), a double-breasted suit with splashy, wide tie.

beach-themed dolls exemplified the new tone of the decade both in Western society and in Barbieland, they were not the first Barbie dolls to engage in sports. Barbie's first sport was fishing. "Picnic Set" (1959–1961) was composed of blue jeans, gingham blouse, straw hat trimmed with flowers, frog brooch, and cork wedgies. Barbie carried a basket with a gingham hanky, a tiny bamboo pole with nylon line and sinker, and a sunfish dangling from the end. She'd have another fishing pole and catch in 1973 with the "Barbie Going Boating Set."

In 1962, Barbie and Ken wore tailored "Tennis Anyone?" outfits, proving their facility on the court and symbolizing the perfect "couples" sport. But they also shared lots of other sports together. For ice skating, Barbie had the typical white furry chubby matched with a tiny red velvet skate skirt, beige hosiery, and impeccable white skates just like the ones seen at the Rockefeller Center rink. Ken wore "Fun on Ice," a gold and blue argyle sweater, corduroy pants, and a gold cotton jersey cap with a pompom. Mittens and a scarf completed his outfit. In 1965, Barbie's outfit would be updated with "Skater's Waltz," with a furry hat, mittens, and short pink jersey dress.

"Ski Queen" and "Ski Champion" took the couple to the snowy slopes in splendid examples of contemporary sportswear of 1963, complete with skis and ski poles.

Ken ventured into boxing competition with "Boxing Outfit," complete with gloves and satin shorts. He wore "In Training" in 1961. The package text for this outfit enthused: "Ken shows how he earned his team letter! He works out daily in a knit tee shirt and elastic-waist boxer shorts. His exercise manual and dumbbell set help him keep trim." Ken also wore "Playball," to meet the Mets. "Sportsman" and "Morning Workout" were accessories for baseball, with a tiny wooden bat, baseball mitt, dumbbells, razor, scuffs, and a telephone to call the gym to see if it was open. "Going Bowling" reflected one of America's favorite pastimes. Regrettably, it did not come with a bowling ball.

"Hiking Holiday" (1965) and "Mountain Hike" (1966) were the last sports outfits for Ken before he temporarily walked off the scene, literally deciding to "take a hike," only to return later to lots of sports adventures. Or perhaps Ken drove off in his "Racy Hot Rod," created by Irwin Corporation for Mattel in 1963. It was a hopped-up, stripped-down Kustom Kar with exposed chrome engine, à la George Barris, the wizard who brought to TV the Munstermobile and the Batmobile.

By the seventies, Barbie and Ken were playing golf with appropriate equipment and outfits, riding bikes and motorcycles (Barbie's was pink, of course!). They also drove many different sports cars. In 1962, Barbie acquired her first sports car. It was an orange-pink (the color of Bayer's children's aspirin!), with aqua bucket seats, and, of

Like Barbie, Ken resembled some of the era's sexiest stars. Here's Superstar Ken, looking alarmingly like Robert Redford, wearing "Play It Cool" (1970).

Now Look Ken (1976; *near right*) looking like a cross between Warren Beatty and Neil Diamond, wears "Rally Gear" (1970), a very California casual outfit, which included a short brown leather jacket and cowboy boots. A recent Black Ken *(far right)*, looks very *Mod Squad* in a bell-bottomed denim outfit from 1970.

course, it was a convertible. The spoke wheels and chrome dashboard made it look like a Porsche or Karmin Ghia. "Classy Corvette" (1976) was Barbie's "sleek 'n sporty roadster."

Barbie had always epitomized the healthy, athletic girl-next-door style. For the next several years, there would be variations on this "fun in the sun" theme each year. The dolls engaged in virtually every sport. Mattel provided them with motorboats, tents, pools, sailboats, and equipment for all manner of winter as well as summer activities, outdoor as well as indoor sports. Even Skipper, after ice skating, roller skating, yo-yoing, horseback riding, baseball playing, and skipping rope, had her own gym (1972). Why not? She already had a convertible sports car (Wards, 1965). She eventually would become "Superteen Skipper" with a violet and shocking pink crash helmet and racy-looking skateboard. She'd zoom around with her own muscular boyfriend, Scott.

Nineteen seventy-four saw the "Sports Set" dolls and newcomer Yellowstone Kelley. The series included Sun Valley Barbie and Ken, Newport Barbie, and the new redheaded Kelley. They were "Today's Teens in Outdoor Scenes!", according to their packaging. By 1976, Barbie and Ken were ready for the Olympics. Olympic Barbie looked like the Malibu Barbie, with long, streaked straight blond hair and a new smiling tan face. "Our U.S. Olympic favorite!" claimed the 1975 promotional doll that was used to inform the public of the two-year advertising association with the Olympics. There were several other "Gold Medal" dolls: Barbie Skier, Barbie Skater, Ken Skier, and P.J. Gymnast, with her own balance beam to "make her do daring feats."

There were many official U.S. Olympic outfits separately available, such as Barbie's "Olympic Warm-ups," "Olympic Parade," "Ken's Olympic Hockey" and "Olympic Outfit," and Francie's "Olympic Outfit," as well as one for Skipper. "Olympic Skating" and "Olympic Gymnast Set" allowed the dolls to do "graceful, daring fantastic feats of gymnastics on the high bar." "Barbie's Olympic Ski Village" had its own ski slope and lodge with a fireplace.

"Sporting Barbie" from Italy (1979) had horseback riding equipment and tennis accessories. Also her yellow and white satin outfit was a great golf fashion in the style of Eric Jacobson for David Smith, the foremost name in golf apparel at that time. Her packaging really expressed the whole mood of the times in claiming that "She's a Girl of the 70's who loves Active Sports!"

Sports peaked in 1975, when the "Free Moving" dolls were introduced. They had the capacity to accommodate all the new movements necessary to play sports. Free Moving Barbie, Ken, and P.J. could swing a golf club or tennis racket, and move to dance and exercise. New friends included Curtis and Cara, two new black dolls. The "Free Mov-

It's a "Wild West Adventure" when Barbie and Ken sing country songs on this recording of their vacation at Bar B Ranch.

ing" technology, controlled by a tab in the back, allowed the dolls to move more gracefully and realistically than they had previously. Barbie's posability was, of course, always based on the acceptable social movements of the time.

Sports did not eclipse Barbie's other talents. By 1972, the TV set that came with "Busy Barbie" had our heroine starring in her own show, wearing "Silver Serenade," an aqua and silver lamé knit gown, complete with glittering aqua boa, silver gloves, and a microphone. Also available were three "Fashion 'N Sounds" sets, which came with records of Barbie singing with appropriate outfits. "Country Music" included a festive Grand Ole Opry peasant skirt in ruffles and rickrack, with a crocheted fringed shawl and white knee-high boots. The popularity of country music by such musicians as Johnny Cash and Dolly Parton influenced the creation in 1981 of Western Barbie, Ken, and Skipper. They had fringed outfits, lassos, and sheepskin suede vests. Barbie even sported heavy blue eyeshadow and a big hairdo. A few of her outfits from the "Designer Western Fashions" even recalled Loretta Lynn.

Other changes took place in 1972. Mattel altered its marketing approach. Outfits were no longer given names, perhaps because *haute couture* had phased out this practice. However, the last named sets were amazingly witty: "Bubbles 'N Boots," "The Zig-Zag Bag," "Fancy That Purple," and "Midi Mood" (a reference to the last-ditch effort to dictate hemlines) were names that paid homage to the times. Labels in clothes and the little fashion booklets were discontinued. "Best Buys," the

Barbie was sometimes more formal about her horsemanship. Her "Riding in the Park" (1966–1967) costume came complete with jodhpurs, ascot, brown gloves, tailored tweed jacket, crop, hat, and Lobb-style boots, recalling Dolores Guinness in *Vogue* feature stories. Only the essential parts of the outfit are shown here on a German equestrienne Barbie. Her horse, Dancer, had his own stable.

The BELL HEIRS — California Sun

In 1971, the Malibu dolls arrived on the scene—easygoing, tan, very California. Sensational Malibu Barbie had long, straight blonde hair, while Malibu Ken had molded golden locks. Barbie as sun-worshipper also came as Funtime Barbie, Sun Lovin' Malibu Barbie (with tan lines), Trinidad Barbie (1982, Italy), California Barbie (also 1982, Italy), and Sun Gold Malibu Barbie (1984). All their friends come in Malibu-style, too, including Malibu Christie *(right)* and Malibu Francie *(opposite)*.

1955

39c

WHITMAN ®

malibu
Francie ™
Doll
Book

A WHITMAN® BOOK
Western Publishing Company, Inc.
Racine, Wisconsin
Produced in U.S.A.

In 1966, Francie was
featured on the
cover of *Barbie*
magazine *(right)* as
Barbie's 15-year-old
tomboy cousin, the
"Happiest, Hip-est,
Doll in Town." By 1971,
she reappeared as
Malibu Francie
(above) looking
slightly more "hip"
than she had five
years earlier.

equivalent of pak items, were introduced. They were a budget line of fashions with no accessories or shoes. The focus was on dolls.

But what dolls they were! Walk Lively Barbie and Ken had a new friend, Walk Lively Steffie, a brunet. Living Fluff (1974) was Skipper's new friend, who resembled Skooter. She came with a skateboard, as did Living Skipper. The "Busy" dolls, Barbie, Ken, Francie, and Steffie, had a new mechanism that allowed their hands to open and close. They came with accessories to carry—a portable TV, a suitcase with travel decals, a phonograph with Barbie's hit records, a tray for drinks, and a telephone. The dolls' fashions were of the new dream material, denim, the signature fabric of the 1970s. Barbie wore the very fashionable denim halter top with ruffled patchwork skirt. Patchwork, gingham, and country prints were made the vogue in part by Gloria Vanderbilt. She would lend her name to denim jeans, as would Calvin Klein and Sergio Valente. For her part, Steffie wore a tube top under suspenders, another discovery of this period.

The three talking versions of Busy Barbie, Ken, and Steffie were novel, too. Talking Busy Barbie wore the controversial hot pants, the *clin d'oeil* creation of Tommy Roberts of "Mr. Freedom" in London. They were electric blue satin with attached bib, and were combined with a red nylon blouse, visored headband, green vinyl belt, and green knee-length, moderate platform lace-up boots. "There's a new rock show on TV" was the sort of thing she said.

The next few years were definitely representative of the times. Mod Hair Ken, in 1973, was an unusual breakthrough in terms of acceptable images for Barbie's world. Ken now had shoulder-length rooted hair. He came with reusable hairpieces, including a beard, long Joe Namath–style sideburns, and two macho moustaches. The issue of long hair's acceptability was finally resolved. If Ken could have it, the whole world could. Jim Morrison of the Doors and, of course, the Beatles had long hair. So did all the men in the fashion photos in *Gentlemen's Quarterly* and *Esquire*.

By 1974, Ken was packaged by Montgomery Ward in the "Get Up 'N Go Tuxedo," which made him look as if he'd be welcome in any catering hall in the country. The ensemble, which captured the seventies' acetate large-lapel look, had a shopping-mall aura that could be felt a mile away. Ken could certainly escort the "Quick Curl Miss America" doll (1973) to any event. She wore a bleached white nylon gown with a gold lamé bustier and a bright "Miss America" ribbon. The plastic roses, crown, and scepter indicated that she was ruling.

In 1976, the dazzling "superstar Barbie era" began. The term *superstar* was invented by Andy Warhol for his Factory actress Ingrid, and is supremely appropriate for the world's most adored

mass-produced couple. Barbie's logo changed to a rather corporate style with a purple shadow under it. Packages were color-coded pink. For the first time since the Malibu Barbie, this doll had a big smile, accentuated with dimples. Her arms bent the way a little girl would imagine a glamorous superstar to pose: one hand on the hip and one on the head, brushing the hair back. Superstar Ken looked a lot like Robert Redford in a Las Vegas–act jumpsuit of blue polyester. His dimples and "Ultra Brite" smile were perfect for camera close-ups. The most common reaction to this new Ken was "too macho," but perhaps this is what being a superstar is all about. There have been other superstar personalities in Barbie's world, such as Kate Jackson, Donny and Marie Osmond, as well as their younger brother Jimmy, Kristy McNichol of *Family* TV fame, and Debby Boone, singer and daughter of Pat Boone.

In 1976, the American Bicentennial included fireworks, tall ships, and innumerable promotions in red, white, and blue. Barbie and Ken took part in the celebration in quaint costumes done in colonial-style prints of sentinels and stars. Barbie's Betsy Ross dress had lace trim, Skipper's aproned outfit matched Barbie's old-fashioned granny gown, and Ken wore a patriotic jacket.

Barbie "related" to the seventies perfectly—an active, lively outdoor life, yet always with it and full of fun. Never one to sit still though, Barbie was ready to "blast off" as the decade turned.

Donny and Marie Osmond, sometime superstars, immortalized as dolls.

Love,
Barbie & Ken

The real "Superstars." Dream Date Barbie and Ken reflect the "Superstar" ambiance, with Barbie wearing a gown in her signature pink, and Ken modeling a perfectly coordinated tux. Barbie also had other Superstar gowns, including one in black and silver glitter Lurex with a boa assorti. Superstar Ken wore a tank watch, chrome aviator glasses, a silver graduation ring, and a signature belt buckle. He also had permanently bent arms, supposedly to enable him to hold Barbie's waist when they made big entrances at Hollywood premieres.

Barbie Is Now!

Look who's blasting off on a new adventure! Astronaut Barbie is a sensation in any galaxy. She's dressed for first class space travel in her hot pink and silver metallic top with matching hot pink pants, clear plastic bubble helmet, and back pack.

he new decade featured more exciting trends in which Barbie and her friends participated. Astronaut Barbie (1986) was designed during the period when the space shuttle was being successfully launched and the Columbia went on a daring mission to repair a satellite in orbit. The renewed enthusiasm for space travel would generate a new mood of hope for future adventures in space. An idea was in the air that *2001, Space Odyssey,* and the *Star Trek* movie (not to mention *Star Wars*)

117

Barbie's 1965 "Miss Astronaut" outfit in its packaging.

might one day be a reality. Astronaut Barbie expressed this dream. This intergalactic doll came with a computer keyboard, flagpole and flag, space maps, Astronaut Barbie certificate, and a child-size version of the emblem and flag. She also carried a very "designed" purse that looked as if it were from Fiorucci and on its way to a party in Rome rather than to the moon. Even the logo on the packaging was typeset in NASA-style lettering. Barbie's costumes were very Thierry Mugler–inspired, with silver vinyl maxicoats, exaggerated shoulders, silver polka-dotted white miniskirts, and hip-length boots. The outfits had wonderful names such as "Welcome to Venus" and "Galaxy à Go-Go."

For the "Barbie on Tour" advertisement, the text read: "Join Barbie doll on a space fantasy as she goes space walking, observes Halley's Comet, saves Earth from threatening asteroids, and plants the flag on a newly discovered world."

Barbie was also keeping up with the newest entertainment fads. There has been a rock singer (Barbie and the Rockers) and recently even a Jane Fonda–like Great Shape Barbie. The early eighties saw the roller skating craze sweep America, so Rollerskating Barbie was created in 1981. She wore shiny black satin shorts, just like what everybody was wearing. People were becoming champions on wheels at the chic new roller discos that were popping up everywhere. Since Ken had a matching costume, the pair could compete in championships and blow their whistles to the disco beat.

Ken in the eighties was more realistically grown up than ever. The new Sport 'N Shave Ken was accompanied by shaving gear to shave his moustache or beard, which he could "grow" with a brown marker. All Star Athlete Ken had rooted hair and a metal armband that could pop off his heavily muscled arm as he lifted weights.

Nineteen eighty-five saw a "Day to Night Barbie" emerge. The theme of Barbie in the eighties is "We girls can do anything," which seems to say it all. She is an active businesswoman by day and a glamorous fun-loving woman by night. She comes with a computer as well as a calculator, credit card, business card, and international daily newspapers and magazines. (Ken is on the cover of what looks like *Time*.) All her accessories fit into an attaché case. Barbie wears a pink suit that turns into a frothy evening dress, just as "Twice as Nice" fashions doubled their play value. She proves that she is resourceful and conscious of her clothing budget.

Like today's woman, the current Barbie is pioneering, diverse in her interests, expressive, and feminine. She represents a woman challenged by new ideas and life's broad range of possibilities. Today, in addition to being a rock star, business executive, and astronaut, Barbie is also a veterinarian, journalist, scuba diver, and movie star.

Barbie's world has profited from the boom in high technology. She and Ken have Sony Walkman stereos, a rotating microwave carousel, and a "Hot Rockin' Van" complete with cassette deck. Barbie owns an open electronic piano, which is worlds away from the fussy fake classical instrument she was provided with in 1964 by Suzy Goose Toy Company. This early model had its own candelabrum and Victorian framed portrait of Ken, and played "I Love You Truly" when it was wound up. Her new electronic piano is a sleek decorator type that looks as if it can play anything.

With so much experience and fun behind her, does Barbie ever want to settle down and get married? Since she didn't wed Ken in the early 1960s, she might now marry Bob, her official boyfriend in Brazil. She recently confided that "One day, I shall get married and have a family of my own. It must be really great looking after your own baby! I think I shall enjoy getting married and having a baby of my own."

Barbie's friends, Tracy and Todd, seemed to have enjoyed getting married recently. They were packaged as a bride and groom with their own wedding day play pak that contained a tiered wedding cake, punch bowl, wedding album, and gifts including the perennial toaster.

Picking up on the marriage theme, in 1985 Mattel introduced the Heart Family, a happily married couple with two small children. Mrs. Heart can choose to be pregnant, since she is provided with a maternity dress. The set even includes a tiny newborn and a birth certificate. The Heart Family represent the ideal family with all the accoutrements: a sheepdog, a bicycle built for two with little seats for the children, and, of course, layettes, bassinets, and diapers. For years people have asked why Barbie never got married and had a baby. Now the Heart Family fills this need.

The story of Barbie's production in Japan ex-

Tropical Barbie with her friends Ken, Miko, and Skipper.

Barbie and the Rockers singing "Born With a Mike in Our Hand." This song couldn't be more true since Barbie also had a microphone that came with her famous gown "Solo in the Spotlight" in 1960.

plains a great deal about her later life. Mattel originally produced Barbie in Japan, and all the early Barbies are marked "Japan" on the bottom of one foot or on their boxes. In this country, Barbie had a number of ensembles that were never available in the United States or Europe, including, of course, a kimono, as well as a Chanel-style suit and marabou-fringed shift à la Balenciaga. By 1970 there were different versions not only of the current Dramatic New Living Barbie but of her new friend Ellie, available only in Japan.

In Japan, the Barbie and Ken relationship and lifestyle were so minutely detailed that one could learn much about the international attitude to Barbie. The illustrations for Japanese Barbie and Ken also presented miniature versions of a fantasy teenage life. Barbie was dressed to go to New York, London, Paris, Rome, or Beverly Hills. The Japanese collection by Takara offered such specific Western trends as high-top sneakers, a lab coat à la Fiorucci for Ken in bright plaid, baseball caps, and a "Candy Pop" pop art series.

Takara Barbie, as she has come to be known, had endless accessories, clothes, gift-set jewels, and furnishings. Takara Ken looked like a very young boy. He had reddish blond rooted hair and glasses, and was described as "a lively high school boy of eighteen . . . and a captain of the basketball team." He was available with such accessories as a highly detailed bike, a tank watch, a blazer with heraldic patch and bronze coin buttons, and a duffle bag in leather and plaid.

Many of the Japanese dolls, such as Francie and Skipper, did not look like their European and American versions. The Francie doll resembled the Barbie that was produced by Mattel and Takara in 1980. She was much more innocent and childlike than her American version, with large round eyes and bangs on a round face. This doll looked very much like "Candy," a popular TV cartoon in Japan.

From Barbie's Japanese packaging one can learn intimate details about the doll. She has blood type A. She is 165 cm tall with an 83 cm chest, 58 cm waist, and 83 cm hips. She was born in Los Angeles. (She must have moved when she was a baby to Willows, a town in the Midwest, because she lived there as a teenager, according to all the Random House stories.)

Recently, Mattel and Takara discontinued their licensing agreement. Takara renamed the Barbie sculpting Jenny-Lifestyle Coordination. The new Mattel Barbie in Japan is made by MABA, a joint venture of Mattel and Bandai and a design house named Base Brainwork. The new Barbie has four major incarnations: City Barbie, International Barbie, Resort Barbie, and Princess Barbie. These dolls are as extensive in accessories as all previous dolls, and include such extraordinary details as diamond crosses and pendant jewelry, lace-trimmed straw hats, working zippers in garments, highly detailed furniture, porcelain tea sets, a metal ice bucket, complete with chilled wine and miniature crystal stemware, as well as alarm clocks, working lamps, a series of realistic-looking foods, and minute replicas of perfumes, lipstick, and other cosmetics.

. . .And On

Barbie seems to have enjoyed every trend in all areas of culture and aesthetics for the last twenty-eight years. But there are some areas that are foreign to her. Barbie never had a pet rock. Nor did she have a mohawk or a stud bracelet, like the girls in London a few years ago. She never had a T-shirt with a political slogan or announcement of any kind of liberation. She never went streaking. She never smoked cigarettes (with or without a holder) or wore 14-karat-gold false fingernails. Barbie never wore Rudi Gernreich's topless bathing suit. She did, however, have bell-shaped skirts with the same print as that on her college bedspread, a triumph of personal style.

In a more glamorous mode, a very rare limited edition Barbie Mink was available in Japan. She wore a basic black dress, pearls, black hosiery and flats, and a three-quarter-length gray coat of *real* mink. The outfit was housed in a black lacquered plastic plinth under a display case of lucite. Barbie had a mink also in 1965—a Sears Exclusive.

Over the years Barbie acquired a number of establishments where she could be an employee, proprietor, or client. The "Barbie Fashion Shop" (1962–1964) came with a fashion stage, a vitrine for accessories and club chairs for clients. It had a decidedly Beverly Hills salon atmosphere, complete with striped awning and topiary in jardinieres printed on the outside.

Barbie could also work in a "Fashion Boutique" (1971–1972) and "Fashion Plaza" (1976), which included a moving escalator and four fun departments. The plaza was a "big, busy store!" in which a bevy of Barbies could run amok shopping.

Barbie's "Café Today" (1971) was very mod, covered in graffiti such as "Rock," "Now," "Love," and "Soul." There was a Coke dispenser and Italian designer-look chairs and tables.

More recently, Barbie and Ken served at her own McDonald's (a very special franchise) with its own mini Big Macs and McDonald's architecture. In Europe Barbie now has "Dream Stores" with their own shopping bags. At one moment during her prime years, she wore "Rosy Morning" lipstick, which says it all. Whatever she was doing, she faced each day with "Rosy Morning" lipstick, and life for her was a challenge eagerly anticipated.

Barbie®
Ken
Midge™

TEEN-AGE FASHION MODEL

MATTEL INC. TOYMAKERS®

バービー・ファッションジャーナルVOL.9(1985.1)
●おしゃれなティーンのファッション・リーダー●

Barbie®

バービー通信
バービーのBOY FRIEND Ken 紹介

FASHION LINE UP!
CASUAL BARBIE
FRUITY KISS
BARBIE'S FRIEND
LYCEENNE FLORA

FASHION TOPICS
SCENERY SERIES

POST BOX
●バービー情報

FASHION JOURNAL VOL.9

創作・著作物 ©TAKARA CO LTD 1981,1985
Made under license from MATTEL
INC. TM used under license

The extremely
successful
Japanese Barbie
dolls. *Opposite, top
left:* Barbie, Ken, and
Midge as they looked
in Japan in the early
1960s. *Opposite,
bottom left:* The
Takara Barbie dolls
from the 1980s
licensed by Mattel.
These dolls had many
outfits not available
in the United States,
including, of course, a
kimono. They appeared
much more childlike
than their American
counterparts.
*Opposite, top and
bottom right and this
page:* The MABA
Barbie dolls, 1986.

Barbie's friends and family followed her happy example. When Skipper, in an early commercial, was posed sitting in a high-heeled shoe, it was no ordinary shoe but an exquisite Roger Vivier pump with his signature curved heel. Dreariness and ordinariness simply do not exist in Barbie's world. As the introduction to the Panini *Barbie Sticker Album* explains:

Barbie is seen as a typical young lady of the twentieth century, who knows how to appreciate beautiful things and, at the same time, live life to the fullest. To most girls, she appears as the ideal older sister who manages to do all those wonderful things that they can only dream of. With her fashionable wardrobe and constant journeys to exciting places all over the world, the adventures of Barbie offer a glimpse of what they might achieve one day. If Barbie has a message at all for us, it is to ignore the gloomy outlook of others and concentrate on all those carefree days of youth. Whatever lies in store will come sooner or later. If you stay close to your friend Barbie, life will always be seen through rose-tinted glasses.

Barbie's life has sometimes been criticized as unrealistic—*too* accomplished, *too* glamorous. This idea is very silly; to accuse a fashion doll of not being realistic is pointless. Barbie has represented not only the glamorous woman, the active sportswoman, and the assertive businesswoman. She has also had mundane jobs, such as being a McDonald's waitress, a Pepsi-Cola waitress, and, of course, a baby-sitter, as well as an assortment of temporary jobs. Many of Barbie's jobs have been extensively written about in *Barbie* magazine, in the Barbie novels during the mid- to late sixties, and in games like her "Keys to Fame" game (1964), which included all the early career-oriented costumes.

Speaking of games, the famous "Queen of the Prom" Barbie game of 1961 was "A fun game with real life appeal for all girls." In this game, the players "shop for a formal" and get a choice of dating (in addition to Ken) either Tom, with his smart-looking horn-rimmed glasses and brown hair, or smarmy-looking Bob, with his platinum blond flattop and crew-neck striped sweater. One can only wonder if this Bob was Bob Williams, Midge's first boyfriend, who appeared regularly in the Random House Barbie series, or if he was Barbie's Brazilian boyfriend, who entered Barbie's world much later. As a final date choice, there was Poindexter, the beady-eyed supposed nerd. He actually must have been a time bomb of emotions, poor ol' Poindexter. He was either the cute underdog, remembered for his innocent look and orange hair, or the ultimate failure as husband material.

When a group of friends of mine played "Queen of the Prom" at the Essex House Hotel one evening, Benjamin Liu, a.k.a. Ming Vase, the performance artist, was thrilled to be going to the prom with Poindexter. He credited his sensitive date with helping him win the game. Benjamin couldn't lose with "Enchanted Evening," Barbie's most expensive gown at sixty-five dollars, *and* being president of the drama club. Best of all, he drew a "Surprise" card and was informed that Poindexter wrote a poem about him and won ten dollars, which he insisted on splitting with Benjamin, thus toppling the game in his favor.

But Barbie's life has not been all a game. She worked hard to become the Renaissance woman that she is today. In a 1964 Random House Barbie story, it is revealed that "Barbie had to be an example of strength and courage, but alone in the dark, she could be as frankly lonely as she felt." Through her efforts to be brave and carry on, Barbie earned success. In spite of her many accomplishments, Barbie has also had moments of fear and self-doubt. As David Bowie sings in "Young Americans": "Well, it ain't that Barbie doll / Her heart's been broken just like you." Barbie has always had to make ethical decisions, and has made them, always with a desire to do the right thing. It is no wonder that she is included in the collection of the Smithsonian Institution in Washington.

If Barbie should ever be accused of being a bad influence, the true judges of that would be children. Recently, a *Scholastic News* competition posed the question: "Who was your hero?" Many of the thousands of answers claimed Barbie as the children's heroine. One essay, simply entitled "Barbie," explains: "She has a castle. She is pretty. She is good at playing ball. She is smart. She tells the truth. She has a car. She goes places. She is good to people. She will take you to the store. She is happy." There is no mention of her being too difficult to emulate. There is no reference to breasts or race. Children are cooler than they are credited with being.

If Barbie should be called "too white bread, too Californian," one has only to remember that in the early 1980s the International Barbie dolls were introduced. Barbie now hails from South America, Spain, Hawaii, Italy, France, England, Switzerland, Iceland, and Sweden. She is Oriental, Scottish, Peruvian, and Eskimo—and a host of other nationalities and races. Black Barbie is "beautiful," as her package claims. She wears African-inspired jewels and an afro pick. Barbie crosses boundaries and is symbolically the universal woman; on an even bigger scale, her world with Ken is that of the whole human race.

Barbie has been referred to in every sort of creative expression. As far back as 1965, Erma Bombeck complained in her usual witty way about the never-ending flow of Barbie's outfits and the hopeless battle of trying to avoid buying them for her daughter. In recent years, Barbie has been satirized by Whoopi Goldberg, the black comedienne, and sung about by pop star David Bowie.

She is the center of the plot of the hit film *Weird Science*, starring the sensuous model-actress Kelly LeBrock.

There were rumors at one point that Linda Evans of *Dynasty* was the original inspiration for Barbie, probably the cheap idea of a publicity agent. *The Barbie Project* was an off-off Broadway event that focused on pop culture, using the doll as its symbol. There were even a few designers who copied, line for line, vintage Barbie doll costumes, taking advantage of nostalgia for the sixties and seventies. The "Doonesbury" cartoon invented a parody of the yearly thematic Barbie dolls by concocting the concept of "Fat Barbie," a doll that was easier to emulate than "real" Barbie.

Barbie has been painted by many young new-wavish artists who definitely project her as a sym-bol of their past. She has also been portrayed by some of the world's most fabulous artists, chiefly Andy Warhol. Warhol's ultra portrait of Barbie, created especially for "The New Theater of Fashion," is a masterpiece of pop imagery, *groovy to the max*. What more can anyone say? Warhol, in addition to painting this *clin d'oeil* portrait, played an indirect but extremely important role in the recognition of Barbie as an important symbol. Having inspired the "pop" generation to feel liberated to express such irreverent and poetic glorification of everyday experience, Warhol's magical and humorous eye saw the possibility of "Barbiemania."

Other artists who have interpreted the Barbie doll phenomenon and charisma include Christopher Makos, the talented New York portrait photographer. His work is a great medium to portray the Barbie glamor and intrigue. Christopher's column, "Out in . . . ," for *Interview* magazine, has a style all its own. The photos he creates express all the excitement of the current social trends. His portrait of Barbie conjures up the idea of Barbie as a socialite star.

Mel Odom, whose work is featured in "The New Theater of Fashion," grew up with Barbie and has the distinction of owning my *first* Barbie, a brunette Bubble Cut. About Barbie, Mel has remarked in the introduction to his book *Dreamer*, which includes his Barbie triptych, "I grew up a sissy in a small town, and Barbie was forbidden, and very beautiful to me as a child. I finally convinced my parents to buy me a Barbie, but it was a dark secret and a hidden shame." He later elaborated: "The thing about it was that I grew up in a farming community in the south, all the colors were greens and browns. Then I saw Barbie, who was all turquoise and pink. It was a dramatic contrast."

Mel also has many humorous recollections of Barbie, which account for his idea that Barbie is a modern myth. He recounts the time he wrote Helen Busby, of Mattel's public relations, during the early sixties, inquiring as to why Mattel did not make Barbie with wigs. Busby responded by assuring him that Fashion Queen Barbie was in the works, much to his relief. Mel's first "fashion doll fix" was a seven-inch Lilli doll in a tight blue sheath, which, he claims, "created my hankering for Barbie therapy, because you couldn't get clothes for Lilli, and of course clothes are part of the deal." About the TV commercials, he remembered, "They were totally captivating. On Saturday mornings I couldn't budge from the TV set if I thought one was going to come on." Mel, in unison with this author, then commenced to sing Barbie commercials verbatim, with each nuance of the originals.

Many other talented artists were responsible for making Barbie what she is today. Eliot Daniel and Ken Darby, the team who wrote the first Barbie album, *Barbie Sings!*, in 1961, captured the mood of that time perfectly. They had worked together since 1939, writing film scores, nightclub material, hit songs, and TV and radio shows. Ken Darby won two Academy Awards, one for associate conducting on the movie of *The King and I*. Eliot Daniel received two Oscar nominations for Best Songs—"Never" and "Lavender Blue." Among his most famous scores were the themes for *I Love Lucy* and *December Bride*. Together Daniel and Darby won the *Photoplay* Gold Medal for "With a Song in My Heart." This talented team was responsible for the extension of Barbie's personality and the harmonious blend of pop culture trends with the Barbie image.

Other people responsible for Barbie's image have been her illustrators. Among the first were Maxime McCaffrey, Susie Mode, Greta Elgaard, and Lucia, who captured all the stylized inspiration from the world's most famous fashion illustrators. The Barbie dolls' poses were completely contemporary and reflected the most current trends. Until 1972, the dolls were illustrated as if they were human. New consumer protection laws initiated at that time made it necessary that Barbie not be shown moving in ways impossible for her to achieve. To accommodate these restrictions, hands were illustrated holding the doll. These drawings were still elegant, and often created by Chris Tuveson at Mattel in a style using solid color fields edged with black lines, a style reminiscent of Peter Max and the 7-Up ads of the early 1970s.

Arnie Fine and Allen Adler, among others responsible for package design for Barbie, created exciting innovations to highlight the new Barbie dolls over the years. Arnie Fine created, among many Barbie packages, the startling modern bend-leg doll boxes with the curved-wall interior, as well as display for gift sets such as "Dinner Dazzle" and "Casey Goes Casual" in the later 1960s. Allen Adler conceived the extended flap and trapezoidal box for the "Free Moving" dolls of 1972 as well as the color-coded packaging of the "Superstar" dolls. The image of Barbie has been enhanced by the packaging, which always created a colorful backdrop for the doll as a personality. As a fashion designer for Barbie, Carol Spencer also made significant contributions to the Barbie image.

The days when Barbie wore white lipstick and had gowns with couture names like "Sophisticated Lady," after Duke Ellington's song, or "Sweater Girl," after Lana Turner, are gone but hardly forgotten. Barbie has become a legend. As far back as 1972, Montgomery Ward re-created an "original" Barbie. This commemorative Barbie was the first reference to the doll's history. It was actually produced in conjunction with Ward's anniversary and their reissue of classic dolls such as Raggedy Ann and the teddy bear. This event indicated the significance of Barbie as an established quintessential doll, a symbol in the minds of the baby boomers of that gleaming ideal one carries one's whole life.

Barbie is more than a doll. She can be seen in every elegant woman. Bianca Jagger, Edie Sedgwick, Maxime and LouLou de la Falaise, Dauphine de Jerphanion, and Diana Vreeland have Barbie qualities. Audrey Hepburn in the film *Funny Face*, as she descends the stairs of the Louvre exclaiming, "I like it, I like it—take the picture," is very Barbie-like. Baby Jane Holzer, Debbie Reynolds, Doris Day, and all the Supremes remind one of Barbie. Jackie Onassis and Elizabeth Taylor, Marilyn Monroe and Penelope Tree radiate Barbie aura. Barbie is really just the personification of femininity, personality, beauty, and style.

"Barbie Bomb," an abstract by artist and fashion designer Stephen Sprouse.

Patrick Sarfati, French photographer, portrays Ken in a style of portrait similar to those in his recent book, *Illusions.*

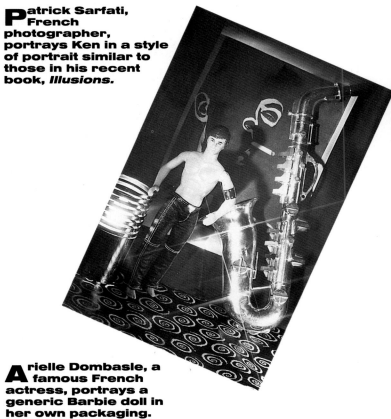

Arielle Dombasle, a famous French actress, portrays a generic Barbie doll in her own packaging.

RENE GRUAU's design for the cover of the French "Nouveau Théâtre de la Mode" catalogue. His drawing of Barbie is pure magic. Gruau is the inspiration for young artists and illustrators everywhere.

Here is "Feelin' Groovy" Barbie, the doll I designed for Mattel U.S. in 1987. For me, she expresses all that was "hip" in the 60s combined with all that is dynamic in the 80s.

PART 2

The New

A COUTURIER'S

Theater of Fashion

SCRAPBOOK

There are no examples left of those dolls that traveled Europe between the Renaissance and the eighteenth century, dressed in the latest fashions. One remembers the day in 1945 when all members of French *haute couture* revived this tradition.

Today, when media allow fashion to penetrate all circles of society, it might seem paradoxical that once again the best representatives of fashion taste resort to a Theater of Fashion. However, while looking at these little long-legged American "girls," we discover in the diversity of their costumes the richness and freedom of contemporary fashion.

Although the fashion world is now international, Paris remains the privileged center for imaginative artisans. Never have their creations appeared more fascinating than when adorned by the magic of miniaturization.

Yvonne Deslandres

curator of the Musée des Arts Décoratifs, Paris

he New Theater of Fashion was inspired by an earlier exposition of fashion dolls, "Le Petit Théâtre de la Mode," presented in April 1945 at the Musée des Arts Décoratifs, Pavillon de Marsan, in Paris. At that time, it was considered quite unusual to present fashion dolls in a museum; but, since the war was just ending, using dolls to show the latest fashions was economical and efficient.

Eliane Bert Bonabel and Jean Saint Martin, when conceiving the idea for the dolls, wanted to convey the image of fashion only through the dresses. They created the dolls in wire and the sculptor Rebull fashioned portraitlike heads of terra-cotta. The hairdos were either curled, braided, flowing, or coiffed and lacquered real hair. Utilizing the talents of embroiderers, *passementerie* makers, artificial-flower creators, feather experts, and button designers, each object was crafted in perfect miniature. Gloves had tiny fingers, parasols opened, handbags had closures that worked, and shoes were actual miniatures with real heels. As with the Barbie New Theater of

Vogue has always been the ultimate in fashion magazines and to be represented within its pages is an acknowledgment of style success for designers, photographers, stars, and models. *Vogue*'s Paris studios, on Place de Palais Bourbon, is often the birthplace of history-making fashion news. Barbie posed there for SERGE RIVIER for an article in French *Vogue* about the New Theater of Fashion.

Fashion, lingerie was executed on the dolls. It would never be seen by the public, but it contributed to the completeness of the idea. For the Stockholm exhibit, furriers made coats in proportion from the finest skins. For the New York exhibit, armed guards were required to protect the dolls' jewels. (The New Theater of Fashion also had armed guards for the entire duration of the show.)

This fabulous decoration was undertaken by the most outstanding artists of the time. Christian Bérard himself painted the faux marble of his opera scenario. Cocteau created a set in his usual controversial style. Others who contributed were Geoffroy, Maclès, Grao-Salla, Wackewitch, Terry, Beaurepaire, Douking, Touchague, Digmimmont, plus thirty-eight hat makers, eight accessory makers, twenty-nine shoemakers, seven furriers, twenty hairdressers, and thirteen jewelers.

The 1945 tour for "Le Petit Théâtre de la Mode" started in Paris and ran for a year and then traveled to Barcelona, Stockholm, Copenhagen, London, New York, San Francisco, Vienna, and Leeds, England. Fifty-three couturiers participated, including Alex, Annek, Balenciaga, Pierre Balmain, Beaujeu, Benoit, Anny Blatt, Bruyère, Calixte, Carpentier, Carven, Chaymont, Dessès, Dhorme, Dormoy, Farell, Jacques Fath, Gabrielle, Gaston, Grès, Heim, Hermès, Issartel, Lafaurie, Lanvin, LeComte, Lucien Lelong, Alix, Manquin, Martial et Armand, Mendel, Captain Molyneux, Montaigne, O'Rossen, Paquin, Patou, Henri de la Pensée, Piguet, de Pombo, Raphael, Madelaine de Rauch, Renal, Nina Ricci, Marcel Rochas, Rosevienne, Maggy Rouff, Schiaparelli, Thomas, Vrament, Vera Boréa, and the Maison Worth. Boris Kochno did the lighting, and Kiffer contributed original drawings.

The New Theater would not have been possible without the magnanimous support of Mattel and the sincere generosity and enthusiasm of the world's most famous couturiers, architects, jewelers, and artists. The show vividly details the evolution of international high fashion and ready-to-wear. And what more suitable mannequin could be found than Barbie.

THE French

DESIGNERS

Yves Saint

It was with surprising pleasure, thanks to Billy Boy, that I discovered the elixir of my childhood again. For it was by making clothing for my sister's dolls that it all began. As one can see, my apprenticeship started quite early, and even though I may have learned a lot since, I can never forget those privileged moments by the Mediterranean Sea, when I first discovered the secret of an art which was to engage my whole life.

I have never seen dolls since without thinking of that period of my life when I believed that clothes were just part of a wonderful game, with colors and fabrics playing together in endless happiness.

I've learned since then how difficult this craft is, because if it gave me many great joys, it also gave me great doubts and anguish. I hope with all my heart that these dolls attract today's children and that they can find, through dolls, the road to their vocations.

—Yves Saint Laurent

For the New Theater of Fashion YVES SAINT LAURENT created a magnificent retrospective of the highlights and innovations of his career. His famous "trapeze" silhouette, made for the House of Dior in 1958, is here represented on Barbie with a gray wool coat dress that first appeared on the cover of French *Vogue* in March 1958.

Barbie's friend Miko models another YSL classic, the pinstripe trouser suit and fedora hat—two fashion breakthroughs.

From Saint Laurent's "Picasso" collection of winter 1979, Barbie wears a black-and-white evening gown.

Laurent

Barbie's interior was exquisitely designed here by the famous decorator JACQUES GRANGE. It is an exact replica of the Saint Laurent couture salon on Avenue Monceau in Paris. Jacques Grange has created actual interiors for many world celebrities and heads of state. Here his homage to Christian Bérard's style is humorously titled "Barbie Forever."

Saint Laurent's long jewel-buttoned evening coat (1979) harks back in feeling to his revolutionary pea coat of 1962.

After the opening of his own house in 1962, Saint Laurent created the now-classic pea coat.

In 1965 came "the dress of tomorrow," the "Mondrian" dress.

140

Saint Laurent's exotic aigrette feather dress *(left)* was modeled by Mounia for the launch of his fragrance "Paris." His cinnamon-colored coat from 1985 *(above)* comes with a floral print gown and was worn in YSL's show by "Miss Africa." Saint Laurent's day dress of printed satin from 1983 *(right)* represents some of the master's most elegant work.

141

Barbie sports the safari outfit of summer 1968, just as Veruschka did in French *Vogue* that year.

From 1980, Barbie wears Saint Laurent's four-piece plaid, impeccably tailored, day ensemble.

From 1976, Barbie wears the magnificent Russian dress, with its ruched underdress and opulent jewels.

Dior

MARC BOHAN, DOMINIQUE MORLOTTI, and FRÉDÉRIC CASTET, three Dior designers, created sublime ensembles for Barbie. Castet, Dior's fur designer, fashioned the full-length lipstick-red mink coat with matching hat and boots, over a black leather dress—a perfect example of Castet's fantasy-making designs.

CHRISTIAN **D**IOR's tradition of classical elegance has been upheld and extended by the mastery of **M**ARC **B**OHAN. For Barbie he created this sumptuous green and black print strapless sheath gown with his significant bustle bow. This gown is an exact miniature of one made for H.R.H. Caroline de Monaco.

Dominique Morlotti, designer of Dior Men's Wear, created a well-known ensemble for Ken *(above)*: slim black leather pants and jacket with "Jules" appliquéd on the back. The character of Jules was made famous by the Jules cologne advertisement illustrated by Gruau *(left)*. Morlotti also created the casual day ensemble *(right)*.

For Ken, Morlotti designed a formal at-home evening robe *(left)* of paisley, which is worn over tuxedo pants. It is finished with a formal shirt with a papillon bow and pearl boutonniere. For afternoon, Morlotti created the plaid suit *(right)* for Ken, which is worn with a pin-stripe shirt and a patterned silk tie. Marc Bohan created Barbie's redingcote dress *(far right)*, which is a miniature of an outfit worn by H.R.H. Caroline de Monaco to the Monte Carlo tennis tournament in 1985.

KENZO's use of color and texture is celebrated internationally. Barbie sports one of his homages to the rainbow. The Japanese-style jacket, closes with frog ties and is combined with straight, wide pants in multicolored stripes. The tremendous hat, tied under the chin, matches the multicolored straw sandals and hair ribbon. Lyrical and happy, Kenzo's outfit sings with good cheer.

Details

Hermès designer ERIC BERGÉRE created for Barbie a travel costume with timeless Hermès detailing and quality: the beige tweed skirt with hand-stitched belt, the turtleneck pullover, the camel's hair coat lined in a Hermès print are accented with a matching hand-rolled scarf, large chain jewels, and equestrian-style brooch. John Lobb–style boots and a hand-stitched miniature travel bag complete the accessories. The "Star" outfit *(left)* from Bergére's recent collection also suggests comfort, elegance, and luxury.

PER SPOOK's couture ensembles for Barbie prepare her for any occasion that calls for casual elegance. For day, he offers a three-piece suit with a loose jacket, striped blouse, and straight skirt, a well-tailored, modern, and lovely style.

ERIC MORTENSEN of Pierre Balmain carries on the tradition of the house with wonderful élan. A blue-black suit with chevron-shaped yoke in pink stripes is coordinated with a raffia cartwheel hat. A fuchsia flower is appliquéd on a strapless black silk sheath. His black and yellow party dress with a triple-tiered ruffled skirt and matching pillbox hat is just right for an evening of dancing. Eric Mortensen's fresh style brings to couture Barbie *ingénuité*. Chignons are by Alexandre de Paris.

MME. GRES's draped and ruched gowns are evidence of her artistic training as a sculptor. For Barbie, she created a sleeveless bodiced ball gown with an enormous skirt edged in blue taffeta. The cut and pleating of the skirt show a splendid mastery of fabric and cultivation of form, as well as a complete understanding of symmetrical balance. The construction and definition of the gown also reflect her perfect attention to detail.

CHRISTIAN LACROIX of the House of Patou presented to Barbie one of the raves of his recent collections. The heavily embroidered heart motif and swirls on the yellow voile blouse are by the famous Francis Lesage. The black sequined cuffs and collar contrast wonderfully with the white satin, tiered fish-tail sheath gown, which, humorously, is cut like jeans! The sequin belt has a rhinestone belt buckle that is repeated in the fabulous coiffure by Alexandre. Barbie carries a crepe shawl in a super shade of mauve.

GERARD PIPART, the designer of Nina Ricci couture, lavished three ball gowns of sheer splendor on Barbie. This one, in black lace, was embroidered by Mme. Brossin de Méré, who designed stylized roses with petals edged in black. The opulence is magnified by the sumptuous pearl and rhinestone jewelry, and the frothy petticoats. The magnificent "belle epoque" hairstyles were conceived and executed by the talented Maurice Franck.

Dear Barbie,

Life is full of unexpected moments, and this exhibition is such a moment. Barbie and her world of perfect dreams, reserved until now for children, has finally invaded the adult world.

If I were a journalist, I would elect Barbie Woman of the Year. Nobody gets so much attention, so many columns in the press, or the opportunity for so many careers. Barbie is even an astronaut as well as a woman of luxury with the most beautiful wardrobe in the world. Designers, painters, photographers have immortalized her, thanks to the imaginative genius of Billy Boy.

We all like to dream, even if the dream becomes rare or impossible to achieve. A miniature dream? Perhaps. But Billy has organized a great exhibition that embodies enthusiasm, generosity, and humor.

Bettina

HANAE MORI'S three ensembles for Barbie show a delicate balance between Eastern simplicity and European high style. Here, Barbie models her white kimono-style gown with hip-level sash, accentuated with pearls; her long, strapless gown of black silk with silver and fuchsia embroidery from shoulder to waist; and her long fuchsia muslin gown with silver and crystal embroidered bustier. Hanae Mori's emphasis on femininity is reflected in her use of color, defined shapes, and gentle flower embroidery.

EMANUEL UNGARO produced four ensembles that display some of his distinctive talents. Ungaro's great flair for mixing prints (he often collaborated with Sonia Knapp on splendid and original prints and textiles) is shown with great imagination in his large-shouldered, wide-collared suit.

LEONARD OF PARIS used one of his dazzling prints to create a marvelous sarong for Barbie.

MARYLL LANVIN of the House of Lanvin created exciting couture outfits for Barbie and the famous Lanvin tuxedo and "academic cutaway coat" for Ken. Ken's hats are by the renowned hat maker Gelot. The embroidery on Barbie's ball gowns is by the extraordinary Lesage.

Among the four ensembles she created for Barbie, JACQUELINE DE RIBES produced a copy of the fabulous gown shown on the cover of *Women's Wear Daily* on April 1, 1985, an Empire-waist sheath in black velvet with sculpted arc sleeves, one in pale ice blue and the other in daffodil silk. The effect implies a great understanding of the clothes women of style and refinement want to wear. Jacqueline de Ribes has also created two soignée gowns of extraordinary colors and intriguing cut, and a day suit of striking proportion.

AGNÈS B. creates classic separates that everyone loves to wear. Versatile cotton shirts, tailored leather jackets, and pullover cotton jersey tops can be worn every day for casual times or a busy workday. For Barbie she created these four outfits that are both comfortable and pretty.

JUNKO SHIMADA made a scintillating skintight sheath of black python skin and a matching big coat, lined and trimmed in white astrakhan. As accessories, Barbie wears matching ultrahigh heels and ropes of pearls, and matching earrings. Her makeup has been highlighted with eyeliner and very red lipstick. Shimada's style is dashing and intriguing.

CARVEN's style is well known for its distinct enhancement of the feminine figure. For Barbie, she created two ensembles for day: bloomer knickers, a blouse with side-tying bow, and a collarless, topstitched box jacket. For evening, a pink taffeta bustier gown with asymmetric bouffant sleeves. A crepe shawl to cover bare shoulders that drapes across the body to tie at the waist. This is couture of simple elegance with a superb accent on color.

MICHEL KLEIN made a kicky, youthful jersey miniskirt and top for Barbie, with a quilted minicoat in bright orange. She wears black tights and has a short hairstyle. The effect is swinging and humorous. Michel Klein designs for the active woman, ready for fun and adventure.

ANDRÉ COURRÈGES invents *the* look of tomorrow, with his "Couple of the Year 2000." In matching cosmonaut outfits of heavy cotton, lamé, and plastic, complete with helmets, these intricately cut garments highlight Courrèges's far-reaching ideas on design. His impeccable attention to chic makes his avant-garde couture ideas complement today's mood. This balance makes the Courrèges look stunning, original, and very beautiful.

Dik Brandsma creates young, playful clothes. *(right)* For Barbie he confected a perky daytime suit. She carries a typical French *baguette* and a copy of *Le Monde.*

For Barbie and Ken, Charvet, the famous clothier located on the Place Vendôme in Paris, fashioned chic outfits for day using his signature shirting fabric.

Pierre Cardin, known for clean-line modern couture, made Barbie and Ken representatives of his sophisticated taste. For Barbie, a stark blue and white crepe suit has a square-shouldered jacket with a becoming detail that folds over and forms a triangle. Accented with rhinestone buttons down the front, it ties with a leather sash. Ken sports a wide-collared leather blouson and skintight pants. They both wear leather headbands. Exciting and full of life, Cardin's style is at once contemporary and timeless.

Just after the Liberation, the French *haute couture*, for promotional reasons, decided to collaborate with a certain number of painters, decorators, and writers, to bring new value to its creation. This is how the "Petit Théâtre de la Mode" was created. The purpose of it was to dress dolls and stage them. Very famous artists participated in this new adventure, which showed, at the time, the creative imagination, the innovation, and the dynamic spirit of our great couturiers. The "Petit Théâtre de la Mode" is part of the history of *haute couture*, of the history of Paris, of history period. . . .

We salute BillyBoy's innovation in reviving this event through the Barbie exhibit that he has organized in Paris, the French provinces, and America. All the innovations which serve the purpose of *haute couture* keep alive the burning passion in the young generations and can only be highly welcomed by our profession, which is always careful to maintain the tradition.

Jacques Mouclier

delegated president of the French Federation of Haute Couture

POPI MORENI created the adorable characters of the commedia dell'arte, including Colombine, Harlequin, Pierrot, and Punch. The effect is quite charming.

CALVIN CHURCHMAN, a brilliant young furniture designer and artist working in New York City, created the scheme for Barbie, cleverly entitled "Portfolio." The precision design, the exquisite realization, and the poetic understanding of the purpose of environment are handsomely demonstrated in this harmonious interior.

ANDREE PUTMAN is marvelous. Her perfect, timely taste is echoed around the world with each new interior she orchestrates. Her contemporary settings, applications and rediscovery of classical twentieth-century furniture, lighting, and interior architecture, become fresh and set new standards of aesthetic purity. For Barbie she created the archetype of her penthouse bathroom at Morgan's Hotel in New York. It is the epitome of glamour and retro high fashion.

SONIA RYKIEL understands line and movement and the kind of clothes that are needed today. Her knit ensembles, which were executed especially for Barbie in Italy, represent these qualities. For example, in navy blue, there are knit jeans with sweaters and beret, wide pants with sweaters and turban, and a superb pleated skirt, banded in yellow, with a turban. Several sweaters are knit with the "6," the street number of her boutique. All show excellently her ease of style. Sonia Rykiel has a wonderful sense of sensuality and texture in her soft, feminine clothes; she adheres to the traditions of quality balanced with comfort.

TAN GIUDICELLI created three outfits for Barbie, including a bouncy, froufrou, polka-dot cocktail sheath, cuddled in a mass of plumes and pinfeathers. A large polka-dot bow provides an amusing back detail that lends charm. His whimsical creation on Barbie is a combination of coquetry and sophistication. All the Giudicelli creations sparkle with his playful party atmosphere.

JACQUES GAUTIER made his representative pale lavender crystal and silver heart pendant with matching earrings for Barbie. He is known for his romantic and poetic creations, which Barbie is now lucky to wear.

JEAN-FRANÇOIS PELLE-GRIN is one of the Rue de la Paix's celebrated high-fashion jewelers, whose refined taste, blended with his extraordinary sense of color and shape, is appreciated by many. He is famous for utilizing unusual stones in clever settings.

JEAN CAZUBON and YVONNE DUDEL have worked as designers for a famous couturier for over thirty years. They created this *luxe* and sophisticated suit for Barbie that reflects their impeccable standards, exacting talent, and knowledge of the most classic *haute couture* methods.

JEAN DINH VAN invented "square jewels," which are copied all over the world. For Barbie, he miniaturized a double link motif necklace to match his famous "square circle" bracelet. He uses pearls and gold in a belt for Barbie that matches his pearl and rounded-square pendant necklace. He shows his famous "rectangular link chain" as well for a belt. A "half-circle" bracelet sparkles with simplicity and refinement. These jewels are pure in line, sober, classic, and attractive. These miniaturized jewels are truly tiny sculptures.

ORLANE made Barbie sensational with a facial and makeup. For the eyes: Bronze Métal and Mauve du Soir. For the lips: Sienne blush, Rouge Ancien. Nails: Très Rouge. All high-quality Orlane products, these. Barbie's salon, painted in Orlane signature colors, is complete with Orlane Skin Repair, Orlane Night Cream, and Orlane Recovery Solution. Barbie even wears an Orlane-created terry bathrobe and headband.

Fabulous designers bursting with style!
A. Thierry Mugler's black velvet and diamond-studded Edwardian coat with matching capri pants;
B. Jacques Loicq's New Wave ensembles for Ken and Barbie;
C. World famous hat-maker Jean Barthet's black straw for Barbie with a screen made by Claude Montana;
D. Jean-Louis Scherrer's Indian-inspired evening ensembles;
E. Herve Leger and Christine Baraldi's fantastic and colorful outfits;
F. Barthet's famous "Umbrella" hat;
G. Phillipe Venet's luxurious silk organza gown decorated with diamanté rhinestones;
H. Barthet's glorious mink and rhinestone hat;
I. Angelo Tarlazzi's "Barbie Berbere," a mysterious Algerian-style gown;
J. Anthony Villarreal's "Liquid Lanterns" gown;
K. Jean-Paul Gaultier's cone-shaped sheath for Barbie and 40s-style suit jacket with matching shirt for Ken;
L. Herve Leger's gorgeous day dress for Barbie;
M. Stephane Plassier's silk pajamas for Ken and his flowered gown for Barbie;
N. A romantic and luxurious chiffon gown detailed with lavish crystal and silver bead embroidery by Phillip Guibourge of Chloe;
O. Alexandre de Paris's coiffure-inspired Empire-style gown;
P. Paco Rabanne's "Body Sculpture";
Q. Christophe de Menil's marigold "scissors skirt" with exquisite accessories based on sea motifs by multi-talented sculptor and designer Claude LaLanne.
R. Jean-Remy Daumas's long-and-short lamé and tulle gown with "gift-wrapped" hat;
S. Bernard Perris's iridescent gown and "Statue of Liberty" costume;
T. Fashions by the students of Mme. Marie Rucki's Ecole Bercot.

A.

B.

F.

G.

K.

L.

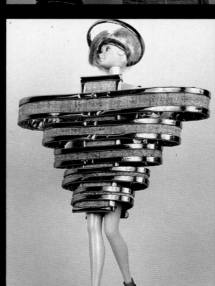

P.

Q.

D.

E.

I.

J.

N.

O.

S.

T.

LOUIS FÉRAUD's youthful and romantic bell wedding dress aptly displays Féraud's superb taste.

These four ensembles by Guy Laroche exemplify his attention to detail and his emphasis on feminine grace. The three day ensembles are perfect for attending any wedding—even a Royal one. The chic suit with a straight skirt of navy wool and tailored jacket of rose wool is accented with contrasting navy lapels, lacquered rose straw hat, and pearl necklace. The drop-waisted blue satin dress is accessorized with an exquisitely draped scarf and navy cartwheel hat. The black bustier sheath comes with a V-neck pink silk blouse that knots at the hip. For a ball, the stunning draped gown of sheer white chiffon creates an alluring effect. In back are two long trains attached with ruby clips. All superb!

GUY LAROCHE celebrates a summer wedding with Barbie as the beautiful bride! His extraordinary gown of white satin has a "butterfly skirt" that comes to the knees. The bodice is of minutely scaled white lace embroidered with spangles. The large white bow ends in a spectacular train. An enveloping tulle veil is accented with a bandeau of diamanté stones and a superb aigrette plume.

FRANCESCO SMALTO created a classical bridal gown for Barbie, a miniature of the wedding gown from his first women's collection, shown on March 24, 1985. The jeweled veil is by Jean Barthet; the drippy chain scarf necklace is by BillyBoy. Barthet and BillyBoy created the same pieces for Smalto's fashion show.

The Italian

NATALIE DU PASQUIER'S interior for Barbie is mod, fun, and cartoonlike. It sets a precedent, as it is the first interior executed in which every detail (including the fabric and carpet) is designed by du Pasquier herself. Her work is full of life, enthusiasm, and elegance.

Designers

JEAN-CHARLES DE
CASTELBAJAC
created his coat in
signature striped
wool. Humor and irony
make these garments
real conversation
pieces. His "Raison
d'etre by Jean
Cocteau" dress and
his large print jacket
for Ken reflect his
great interest in
incorporating art into
fashion.

ENRICO COVERI has a
gift for color and
striking graphic crea-
tions. His sweater with
three-quarter sleeves
matched with swirly
patterned tights is
very candy-colored
and appealing. Coveri
is the leader of "Com-
media Dell'Arte,"
tongue-in-cheek
dressing that results
in stylish, fun clothes.
Barbie jumps for joy
over Coveri outfits.

THOMAS MAIER cre-
ated four swagger-
ing outfits for Ken.
With his interpreta-
tions of the American
baseball jacket, polo
shirt, and jogging
pants, he prepares
Ken for outdoor activi-
ties. Patches with
names, letters, and
numbers decorate his
great casual wear. He
accessorizes the out-
fits with baseball caps,
snoods, hoods, and
ski caps. Slip-on loaf-
ers, felt sneakers, and
a carefully wrought
belt complete the look.
Comfortable and boy-
ish, Maier succeeds in
bringing Americana to
European menswear.

EMILIO PUCCI has been the grand master of extraordinary and artful prints and Italian fashion for more than three decades. His vision is legendary and includes the design of every facet of fashion, perfume, pottery, furniture, rugs, plane interiors, houses, and packaging. His thirteenth-century palace, "Palazzo Pucci," in Florence, is an active center of creativity and exuberance. Emilio Pucci lavishes his talent on Barbie. His signature-print outfits include daytime dresses, evening gowns and capes, and home-entertaining palazzo pants.

LUCIANO SOPRANI cre-
ated a sophisti-
cated belted trench
coat for Barbie, a
classic idea inter-
preted for contempo-
rary taste. Soprani
makes a swaggering,
sultry silhouette to in-
trigue the sartorially
minded woman.

LORIS AZZARO created
for Barbie his
spectacular, entrance-
making sheath gown
of beaded chiffon,
over which he puts
his glamorous coat
of white swan's down
trimmed with beads.
This dress is a pre-
cise miniature of the
one Azzaro originated
for Marlene Dietrich.
Alexandre de Paris
created his fabulous
"Dietrich" coiffure for
Barbie. The total look
is devastatingly chic.

Dear Barbie,

When BillyBoy told me
that there would be an
exhibition in America of
your entire wardrobe, in-
cluding creations by the
most famous designers, I
was ecstatic.

You know, we have
something in common:
our work in fashion. You
are the most beloved doll
ever, and I, before my
film career, was a cover
girl. I know so well the
work of these couturiers,
and I must say, the
clothes suit you beauti-
fully. Of course, being
Italian, I felt proud to
see you dressed by my
dear Valentino, Capucci,
Pucci, Fiorucci, Lan-
cetti, Benetton, Versace,
Rocco Barocco, and Cov-
eri—who, by the way,
also have dressed me.

Elegance has no age.
Thanks to BillyBoy and
the talent of all who have
contributed to the show,
you are passing through
fashion history with grace
and beauty. You are part
of an adventure that will
remain forever in the an-
nals of couture.

*Elsa
Martinelli*

Rome-based Pino Lancetti's couture is renowned for its opulent fabrics and combination of textures, its high standard of couture construction, and the brilliance of Lancetti's designs. His fabulous creations for Barbie bring together the mystery and romance of Rome, with the luxury and elegance of high fashion.

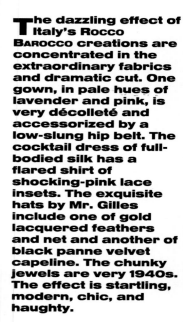

The dazzling effect of Italy's Rocco Barocco creations are concentrated in the extraordinary fabrics and dramatic cut. One gown, in pale hues of lavender and pink, is very décolleté and accessorized by a low-slung hip belt. The cocktail dress of full-bodied silk has a flared shirt of shocking-pink lace insets. The exquisite hats by Mr. Gilles include one of gold lacquered feathers and net and another of black panne velvet capeline. The chunky jewels are very 1940s. The effect is startling, modern, chic, and haughty.

Regina Schrecker, working in Italy, creates a dramatic line of clothes for evening and day. She also designs menswear, knitwear, all sorts of accessories, and her own perfume. Her ensembles for Barbie and Ken reflect her sense of romantic elegance.

CARLO TIVIOLI created sumptuous mink outfits, such as a fur-lined cape coat using bronze leather and a gold leather short jacket ensemble. Somehow these lush creations combined fabulously with Barbie's early "Evening Splendor" and with Ken in his Dior smoking jacket.

VALENTINO, known throughout the world for his exquisite taste and passionate, expressive couture, created the sublime couture gown of multi-layered red tulle ruffles and matching jacket. The Valentino fragrance, in its miniature tasseled flask, rests on the sofa from Valentino Piu. With the Caravaggio print, it altogether makes a vision of the ideal Valentino woman: sensual, feminine, and mysterious. The hairstyle is by the fabulous hairdresser Sergio Valenti.

ROBERTO CAPUCCI'S colorful and sculptural gowns for Barbie are homage to modern ideas in both fashion and the arts. The expressive forms and colors in these gowns for Barbie recall Matisse's portraits of fashionable women.

Los Angeles artist PETER SHIRE's colorful Memphis watercolor of Barbie's house, from 1985.

The BENETTON company made eighteen exquisite miniatures of their fabulous knitwear and sports clothes. Sweaters with tiny Benetton logos came in bright, young colors. Jeans, parkas with fur-trimmed hoods, fringed skirts, and big, comfortable shirts were created with an incredible attention to detail. They truly create "United Colors of Benetton."

WERNER, an illustrator working in Paris and Italy, is known for his stylish and chic illustrations and eye for fashion trends. Barbie is impeccable, dressed for a day of to-the-minute smart looks.

GEORGE SOWDEN is a Milan-based furniture designer. His ideas are known internationally and can be seen with pieces represented by the controversial but nonetheless thrilling group "Memphis," and also with his "Objects for the Electronic Age" in collaboration with Natalie du Pasquier. His humorous and lucid designs are full of color and irony. For Barbie, he designed a new car—completely revolutionary, startling and chic.

THE BRITISH Designers

FREDDY Fox is the designer of millinery in London, by appointment to H.M. Queen Elizabeth II. He is known for smart traditional hats, and for Barbie he created the ultimate bridal ensemble with a veil of white tulle and horsehair mesh, accented with pearls. His full bride's gown in duchess satin is perfect for a stately formal wedding.

CAROLINE CHARLES used crisp pink silk taffeta and iridescent sequins to effect the superb party dress. Caroline Charles creates magnificent clothes that are truly feminine.

WIM HEMMINK of London created two sumptuous gowns: one, entitled "Etoile," full with a lace petticoat, another, a tight sheath to the floor. Sparkling and romantic, these evening ensembles create a magical ambiance.

MURRAY ARBEID created a classic chiffon, sequin print draped evening dress for Barbie. Its light and starry quality is appropriate for any magical soirée.

CAROLINE EAVIS of London created two entrance-making gowns, one of silver sequins, another in pink chiffon exquisitely hand-embroidered with bugle beads. The look is provocative and reminiscent of the 1920s.

ARABELLA POLLEN *(above left)* known for her brilliant use of color, created a fabulous duffel coat and matching skirt for Barbie. MONICA CHONG *(above right)* created a glamorous zipper sheath skirt and lamé blouse, topped by a fur-trimmed corduroy coat. TOMMY NUTTER, famous for his tailored yet high-style suits, created two fabulous outfits for Barbie and Ken *(below).*

JACQUES AZAGURY'S fuchsia and black gown is a beautiful example of couture. The asymmetrical train adds to the slim silhouette. The fuchsia bandeau, knotted in a bow, accents Barbie's short hair.

BODY MAP, the avant-garde English postpunk designers who design sizzling costumes for dancer Michael Clark, created this African print on nylon that turns into a ruffled trapeze dress.

COREY TIPPIN created the group of poetic masks, subtly expressive and executed to perfection.

STEPHEN JONES of London created a marvelous and humorous "Temple of Barbie," including five busts and a "Venus de Milo" Barbie, all of whom are crowned with his famous hats. Stephen Jones has created exciting millinery for such diverse clients as H.R.H. Diana, Princess of Wales, and Boy George. The devastatingly striking creations are from his collection entitled "For the Heart of Woman and the Soul of Man," of winter 1986.

SCOTT CROLLA and GEORGINA GODLEY of London created two of their most successful and renowned ensembles for Barbie and Ken. Barbie wears the "warrior" outfit, made entirely of brocade, a short fitted jacket with princess lines that has a slight peplum and a Nehru collar. Ken wears flattering tapered brocade pants, typical of Crolla, and a striped brocade Nehru jacket.

PERRY ELLIS was a re-
markable Ameri-
can designer, whose
great understanding
of cut, comfort, and
color are unequaled.
His superb knit
"zebra" sweater and
"Delaunay" sweater
are exquisite exam-
ples.

KEITH HARING created two handcrafted T-shirts of his famous "Glowing Baby" motif especially for the New Theater of Fashion. They are both humorous and poignant in their effect. Keith Haring is known throughout the art world as one of the founders of the interest in graffiti art, as his symbolic motifs were originally drawn on the walls of New York City's subways.

AMERICAN designer KATY K. is known for her decidedly western outfits. Here Barbie models a dancing dress that could go anywhere from Dodge City to downtown Manhattan.

KENNETH J. LANE is world-famous for his exotic, unique, and elaborate costume jewelry creations. For Barbie, he designed a fabulous number "à la Josephine Baker," entirely in rhinestones. Coiffed by Alexandre de Paris, who invented Baker's own hairstyle, Barbie is spectacular and shimmering with Lane's original style and panache!

The jersey sports clothes of New York–based BRIAN-SCOTT CARR are worn by many—including Madonna. He made a modern homage to masculinity for Ken that is reminiscent of an eighteenth-century Japanese woodcut. Ken's ensemble is sensual and mysterious.

LEE BREVARD is an American jewelry designer who uses many different elements to create his pieces. For Barbie, a cameo of a German shepherd dog surrounded by four real emeralds and diamanté rhinestones hangs from a bead pendant and is trimmed with fringe and an eagle motif. His *"clin d'oeil"* approach is humorous and pleasing.

MARIPOL, proprietor of the Maripolitan Gallery, is an exciting and humorous accessories designer in New York City who blends black rubber and metal chain link with 1960s and 1970s motifs. Her high sense of irony and her knowledge of the past and present make her work a breath of fresh air in the fashion world. Barbie wears a black linked metal dress that recalls the fast-paced and mod designs of the 1960s, but is updated in its proportions for today's women.

DIANE VON FURSTENBERG's ensemble entitled "High Noon" has a decidedly 1890s American West feel to it. The stylized and beautifully proportioned gown has a wonderful movement and provocative allure. It is a couture garment that reflects Diane von Furstenberg's impeccable attention to detail.

AKIRA's delightful imagination conceived an elaborate costume combining a jumpsuit and brocade coat. The kimono-inspired cut of the coat shows her mastery of fabric and is a beautiful fantasy for Barbie.

PATRICIA RHODES, KANI IKAI, and PRECIOUS LASHLEY of Chicago have created clothes for Barbie that reflect their high standards of construction and understanding of fashion. Rhodes creates her best-selling suede and sequin sheath gown, Lashley her asymmetrical peplumed day suit in green wool, and Ikai a modern Japanese-style silhouette in black and green striped wool jersey cut in a kimono effect.

CAROLINA HERRERA created two marvelous outfits for Barbie. For a modern woman, they are the height of sober elegance. Of exquisite fabrics, these gowns in tones of midnight blue and jet black recall eighteenth-century portrait ensembles.

GIORGIO SANT'ANGELO, one of America's experts on *both* sophisticated and youthful fashion ideas, selects a jersey body suit with a golden beaded fringe skirt for our favorite girl. The airy gold mesh wrap and sparkling rhinestone accessories pull together a great look so Barbie can breeze through an evening of entertainment and parties with friends.

MARY MCFADDEN realized two romantic evening ensembles for Barbie. Both are medieval-inspired. A signature pleated Empire-waist gown is embellished with beads, and a richly embroidered tunic is splendid in silver thread on black. Her style is recognized for its poetry, opulence, and femininity.

BILL BLASS's name always evokes thoughts of high style and quality. For Barbie, he used his signature houndstooth print in an A-line duster coat, over his impeccable angora sweater with softly tailored slacks.

ARNOLD SCAASI, whose name is synonymous with glamorous clothes, created his diamanté-embroidered white velvet gown with full tulle skirt.

The long, well-tailored line of FERNANDO SANCHEZ creations are well suited to Barbie. Pink pleated fabric is used for a gown and matching long coat, and a smart velvet cowl is matched with a lace bodice for another.

GEOFFREY BEENE's shimmering purple sequin football jersey–style gown is a great example of his witty fashion style. The gown is perfectly proportioned and couture-made, which enhances the splendid ambiance that this fashion innovation creates.

189

KOOS VAN DEN AKKER makes couture and appliquéd fabrics in New York City. He is known in America for creating artworks in fabric. This mandarin coat he created for Barbie is an exquisite example of his innate talent for mixing different shapes and textures of suede, lamé, small-scale prints, and weaves.

EUVA is a California-based fashion designer who utilizes lamés and animal prints in a colorful and perky spirit. The "Wild Things" label, designed by Euva, is a collection of kicky party clothes that are ready for any fun occasion. Barbie is ready for dancing and laughing.

PERRY ELLIS's beefeater-style ensemble and suit with short jacket are exquisite examples of his trend-setting and refined taste, and few model them better than Barbie.

This book could not have been done without the generous support and enthusiasm of many people.

The collection could not be the unique thing it is without the extraordinary works of my friends designing and creating art: Akira, Alexandre de Paris, Alexia, Amanda, Sonia Amselleim, Anna, M. Anderson, Murray Arbeid, Madame Austry, Jacques Azagury, Loris Azzaro, Agnès B., Valérie Banon, Christine Baraldi, Eileen Barin, Rocco Barocco, Jean Barthet, Geoffrey Beene, J.F. Beguin, Benetton, Eliane de la Beraudière, Studio Berco, Eric Bergére, Henri Berhgauer, Bernadette, Bill Blass, Marc Bohan, Catherine Bonnet, Dik Brandsma, Pia de Brantes, Chislane Brege, Ariane Brenner, Lee Brevard, Madame Brossin de Méré, Gabrielle Buchaert, Nicky Buttler, Capucci, Pierre Cardin, Madame Carimini, Brian-Scott Carr, Carven, Jean-Charles Castelbajac, Xavier de Castella, Frédéric Castet, Jane Cattani, Catherine, Jean Cazubon, Ingrid de Champfleury, Madame de Chaumette, Caroline Charles, Charlie (in L.A.), Monica Chong, Calvin Churchman, Beatrice Cifuentes, Henry Clarke, Jack Congleton, André Courrèges, Enrico Coveri, Cristina, Scott Crolla, Dauphine, Madame Debize, Debra, Marie-Catherine Delalande, Madame Frances Dievleveult, Jean Dinh Van, Dior, Daniel Dislhaire, Dominique, Michel Douard, Yvonne Dudel, G. Duval, Caroline Eavis, Perry Ellis, Mademoiselle Esther, Evette, David Evins, Euva, Roberto Fabris, Tom Fallon, Madame Felisa, Louis Féraud, Ercilia Fiorucci, Carol Flinch, Heidie Fisher, Frederick Fox, Maurice Franck, Mademoiselle Frédérique, Lady Fretwell, Monsieur Gaby, John Galliano, Jean-Paul Gaultier, M. and Mme. Jacques-Andrée Gautier, Olivier Gelbsman, Monsieur Georges, Monsieur Gilles, Gian Carlo Giametti, Madame Gisèle, Tan Giudicelli, Serge Glon, Georgina Godley, Jean-Claude Gombault, Jacques Grange, Madame Grès, A. Gridel, René Gruau, Sylvie Grumbach, Phillip Guibourgé, Didier Haye, Ves Helse, Wim Hemmink, Hermès, Carolina Herrera, Fred Hughes, Hurel, Isabelle, Madame Jacqueline, Monsieur Jean-Louis, Monsieur Jean-Marie, Monsieur Jean-Pierre, Jean-Claude Jitrois, Stephen Jones, Julie, Carole Julien, Norma Kamali, Béatrice Keller, Caroline Kellet, Kenzo, Michel Klein, Madame Labarthe, Christian Lacroix, Claude Lalanne, Marc Lamour, Pino Lancetti, Kenneth J. Lane, Bernard Lanvin, Maryll Lanvin, Guy Laroche, Hélène Laussière, Brigette Lefèvre, Hervé Léger, Mademoiselle Leonard, Léonie, Francis Lesage, Lillian, Jacques Loicq, Mary McFadden, Thomas Maier, Leila Manchari, Maripol, Christophe de Menil, Hanae Mori, Dominique Morlotti, Eric Mortensen, Thierry Mugler, the "Mums," Craig Natiello, Yves Navarre, Madame Nicole, Jasper Nyeboe, Mel Odom, Orlane, Natalie De Pasquier, Patou, Jean-Francois Pellegrin, Bernard Perris, Gérard Pipart, Stéphane Plassier, Arabella Pollen, Patrick Pradalie, Emilio Pucci, Andrée Putman, Paco Rabanne, Guy A. Rambaldi, Ariel de Ravenal, David Frank Ray, Mr. and Mrs. Stephen O'Reilly-Hyland, Lyn Revson, Jacqueline de Ribes, Nina Ricci, Serge Rivier, Romy, Rosanna, Marie Rucki, Sonia Rykiel, Anne Sailly-Fillion, Bernard Sandoz, Fernando Sanchez, Giorgio Sant'Angelo, Patrick Sarfati, Djamila Saiah, Arnold Scaasi, Jean-Louis Scherrer, Axel Schmitt, Helene Scher, Barbara Schonfeld, Serena, Junko Shimada, Peter Shire, Francesco Smalto, Mr. and Mrs. Clyde Smith, Roberto Snow, George Sowden, Per Spook, Susanna, Angelo Tarlazzi, Gerald Tavenas, Alexandra Tchernoff, Hughes Ternon, Corey Grant Tippin, Francis Touyarou-Gabe, Emanuel Ungaro, Valentino, Koos Van Den Akker, Monique Van Vooren, Phillipe Venet, Gianni Versace, Mademoiselle de la Verteville, Anthony Villarreal, Diane Von Furstenberg, Frank Weill, Werner, Glenn Williams, Rob Wynn, Quentin Yerba, Sophie Xuereb, Bill Anderson, Marilyn Evins, Vincent Knapp, Popi Moreni, Jin Abe, Carolyn Cuadros, Jacqueline Jacobson, Jean-Remy Daumas, Regina Schrecker, Luciani Soprani, Keith Haring, Julia Gruen, Patricia Rhodes, Kani Ikai, Precious Lashley, Katy K., Leonard and Juliette Pennacchio, Charvet and Anne-Marie Colban, Gregory Poe, Christina Banks, H.R.H. Prince Serge de Youboslavie, Joey Arias, Wendy Samimi, Jenifer Corker, Peter Foster, Tirapan Vanarat, Pichitra Boonyarataphan, Chairat na Bangchang, Anon Poungtubin, Somchai Kawthong, Kerati Challasith, Jean-Pierre Masclet.

Special thanks to Yves Saint Laurent, Pierre Bergé, and the Maison Yves Saint Laurent for taking a special interest in my work and this project, and for having been supportive, enthusiastic, and generous from the very beginning; Pat Hackett for her special eye on Barbie; Paige Powell for all her encouragement; Jacques Mouclier, who has been generous with his time and his interest; Yvonne Deslandres, who has been my spiritual mother and has always been behind my work as a guiding force; and to the glamorous Elsa Martinelli and the stunning L.H. for their help and good humor.

I appreciate all of Crown's positiveness. I'm really grateful to Pam Thomas, who really has been fabulous, truly, as an editor and scintillating as a friend. Erica Marcus has been cheery and helpful and wonderful and glamorous. The indefatigable Mimi Morton did a fabulous job refining the manuscript. Also at Crown I'd like to thank the masterful Ken Sansone, the visionary George Corsillo, the regal and witty Amy Boorstein, and the sparkling True Sims Weiser, all of whom helped my book become a book.

I'm sincerely appreciative of the initial support and constant encouragement from Mrs. Jacqueline Onassis of Doubleday, who really got people hopping about this book, as well as Shaye Arehart and Jim Fitzgerald, who have been supportive and gave me excellent advice and direction.

Jeffrey Simmons has been fantastic and has moved mountains.

Mattel, Inc., has been superb, especially Tom Kalinske, Tom Wsalek and Wayne Lynch, Beverly Cannady, Joe Morrison, Harvey Diamond, Jill Barad, John Amerman, Barbara Miner, Gail Susik, Gary Price, Mary Beth Orfao, and the groovy Candace Irving. At Mattel, France, I'd like to thank Robert Gerson and Didier Bodel, Also very helpful were the people at Rogers and Cowen, including Kelly Breidenbach, Holly Howard, and Stephen Spurgeon.

I'd like to thank Lance, artist and friend, for his enthusiasm and his kind loan of the comic books; Pat Timmons, who has been a special Barbie friend; Sarah Eames and Susan Manos and family for their dedication to the Barbie doll phenomenon.

Also, the immediate people around me who were dropped into a psychedelia of Barbie Haze and were overwhelmed by deep Barbie therapy (not necessarily of their own will): Lala, who put up with me and 22,000 pairs of open-toed pumps for years; Jane X, my fabulous and gorgeous "gal friday" and second left hand who, by now, can type Barbie in one quarter of a second and has every single detail about pak-items, harlequin frames, and sheaths deeply ingrained in her subconscious; Bettina, who is a Barbie (nuff said?); Diane Vreeland, whose encouragement has been fabulous; Andy Warhol, who made a Barbie dream come true.

And last, but by no means least, I would like to thank Midge, who really stuck by me through thick and thin.